T0301845

Emotions and Consumption Behaviour

To Giovanni and Francesco,
my beloved nephews

Emotions and Consumption Behaviour

Isabella Soscia

SKEMA Business School, France

Edward Elgar
Cheltenham, UK • Northampton, MA, USA

Published by
Edward Elgar Publishing Limited
The Lypiatts
15 Lansdown Road
Cheltenham
Glos GL50 2JA
UK

Edward Elgar Publishing, Inc.
William Pratt House
9 Dewey Court
Northampton
Massachusetts 01060
USA

A catalogue record for this book
is available from the British Library

Library of Congress Control Number: 2012951756

This book is available electronically in the ElgarOnline.com
Business Subject Collection, E-ISBN 978 0 85793 797 1

ISBN 978 0 85793 796 4

Typeset by Servis Filmsetting Ltd, Stockport, Cheshire
Printed by MPG PRINTGROUP, UK

Contents

List of figures   vi
List of tables   vii
List of boxes   ix
Preface   x
Acknowledgements   xii

1   Consumer emotions and behaviour   1

2   Happiness and unhappiness   25

3   Pride and sense of guilt   54

4   Anger and gratitude   78

5   Consumption emotions and the determination of
    post-consumption behaviour   98

References   117
Index   133

Figures

1.1 Classification of emotions based on arousal and
      desirability   18
1.2 Consumption emotions: cognitive antecedents and
      action tendencies   22
2.1 The influence of relations on consumption happiness   33
2.2 Relationship between consumer satisfaction and
      post-purchase behaviour   39
5.1 Scenario 3: seller-caused outcome X goal incongruence   104
5.2 The questionnaire   105

Tables

1.1	Coping methods	14
1.2	Action readiness methods	16
2.1	Happiness and unhappiness: cognitive antecedents and action tendencies	29
2.2	Happiness: appraisals, actions triggered by appraisals, marketing tactics, action tendencies	35
2.3	Hope and fear: cognitive antecedents and action tendencies	42
2.4	Hope and fear: appraisals, actions triggered by appraisals, marketing tactics, action tendencies	44
2.5	Role played by satisfaction, hope, fear and nostalgia in the purchase and consumption processes	51
3.1	Guilt: appraisals and action tendencies	57
3.2	Consumer guilt: appraisals, actions triggered by appraisals, marketing tactics, action tendencies	62
3.3	Shame and embarrassment: appraisals and action tendencies	64
3.4	Consumer shame and embarrassment: appraisals, actions triggered by appraisals, marketing tactics, action tendencies	71
3.5	Pride: cognitive antecedents and action tendencies	72
3.6	Consumer pride: appraisals, actions triggered by appraisals, marketing tactics, action tendencies	75
3.7	Social emotions during the various phases of the purchase and consumption process	76
4.1	Anger: cognitive antecedents and action tendencies	79
4.2	Possible reactions to customer anger and the resulting post-purchase behaviour	83
4.3	Consumer anger: appraisals, actions triggered by appraisals, marketing tactics, action tendencies	88
4.4	Gratitude: cognitive antecedents and action tendencies	91

4.5 Consumer gratitude: appraisals, actions triggered by appraisals, marketing tactics, action tendencies 95

4.6 Anger and gratitude during the various phases of the purchase and consumption process 97

5.1 The first two research assumptions 102

5.2 Factor analysis 106

5.3 Correlations between emotions and complaining and negative word of mouth 108

5.4 Regression of complaint and negative word of mouth on emotions 108

5.5 Correlations between emotions and repurchase intention and positive word of mouth 109

5.6 Regression of repurchase intention and positive word of mouth on emotions 110

5.7 Step-down analysis (p values of the multivariate F-test statistic) 111

Boxes

1.1	Anticipated emotions	8
2.1	The consumer's affective and cognitive reactions to the social context	32
2.2	Customer satisfaction: various standards in the confirmation/disconfirmation paradigm	38
3.1	Empathy and social consumption emotions	65
3.2	Does trash in advertising work? Disgust and embarrassment used to attract attention	69
4.1	An apology from JetBlue Airways	85
4.2	A sentiment of gratitude by Lafeber Company	96

Preface

Only over the past decade or so have researchers studied the role of emotions in the economy, especially in the field of marketing. This new interest derives from widespread dissatisfaction with current theories and managerial prescriptions with respect to purchase and consumption behaviour, which are typically rational and overly cognitive. The emotional side of consumption seems to play an essential and significant role in explaining choices made and actions taken by consumers. Modern consumers increasingly realize that it is 'experience' that they desire, not so much the physical goods or services per se. But experiences of the right sort require that marketers create a venue for experiences that will arouse strong emotions in consumers prior to and at the moment of consumption and in the period of time following consumption so as to orchestrate the proper sort of positive emotions. At the same time, marketers can achieve some of their goals by the skilful arousal of certain negative emotions, such as anger, fear, or disappointment.

The emotions experienced by a consumer also awaken post-purchase behaviours, such as the decision to repurchase or abandon a brand, and lead to positive and negative word of mouth, complaints, or, in extreme cases, boycotts of a company. Until recently, marketers viewed consumer responses in simplistic ways and relied on narrow conceptions of emotion; namely, satisfaction/dissatisfaction was the sole emotion thought to account for decisions to continue with or abandon a product or a service. However, practitioners as well as academic researchers have come to the conclusion that satisfaction/dissatisfaction is a poor explanation for gaining insights into consumption: a dissatisfied consumer, for example, can both complain and spread negative information about his or her consumption experience or may even decide to abandon the brand or service provider that disappointed them, yet satisfaction/dissatisfaction does not explain which particular reaction will occur. Because each of these three types of negative behaviours has different managerial implications, it is therefore of great importance for marketing managers to be able to anticipate their occurrence accurately, and in turn, require a better understanding of their distinctive emotional drivers, so that marketers can act accordingly.

Precisely to give managers a predictive model that is more useful than that provided by the concept of customer satisfaction/dissatisfaction, in the final chapter of this book I consider a broader, yet more fine-grained framework that can be implemented and tested in the real world. The framework incorporates three psychological concepts that are introduced in the first chapter: cognitive antecedents, emotional responses and tendencies to engage in action. In order to fully understand the distinctive characteristics of the different emotional responses presented, their perceived origins and their relative managerial implications for consumers' goal outcomes, it is necessary to scrutinize how emotions function in consumers, from both a psychological and a managerial perspective. In particular, the second chapter examines the cognitive antecedents and the action tendencies of happiness and unhappiness. The third chapter, in contrast, analyses social emotions, in particular, guilt and pride, which are affective feelings pervading the life of consumers and have important consequences for marketers. The fourth chapter examines anger and gratitude, emotional states that customers experience when they attribute full responsibility for a happy or unhappy consumption experience to the producer or service provider. The central chapters of the volume therefore set out to provide managers with conceptual tools and managerial guidance to prevent certain emotions from arising in consumers or generate desired emotions in consumers and thus inhibit or promote appropriate actions. Again, the last chapter addresses the emotions considered and presents findings from an empirical study testing hypotheses. Managerial implications are also discussed.

Acknowledgements

I would like to express my gratitude to Richard P. Bagozzi for his insightful comments on my ideas for this book. During our in-depth discussions of the book's content, his insights on studying this emotional topic were indispensable.

I am also grateful to Francesco Gallucci for his valuable contribution with regard to emotions and the neurosciences, the section that ends this book and that suggests new, fascinating ways of measuring consumption emotions.

The publishers wish to thank John Wiley and Sons Ltd who have kindly given permission for the use of the following copyright material: Soscia, I. (2007), 'Gratitude, delight or guilt: the role of consumers' emotions in predicting post-consumption behaviors', *Psychology & Marketing*, **24** (10), 874–88.

1. Consumer emotions and behaviour

Studies involving consumer behaviour find their roots in the area of marketing. For this reason, I will first discuss the role played by emotions in marketing before starting to analyse this topic in the context of consumption. It is also indispensable to address the meaning of emotion and to examine the peculiarities of this construct that set it apart from other concepts within the broad category of affect. This chapter ends by presenting a predictive model of purchase and consumption behaviour in the form of a diagram that illustrates the role of emotions in the various phases of the process.

1.1 THE ROLE PLAYED BY THE EMOTIONS IN MARKETING

Precisely due to the managerial relevance of the subject, studies of emotions in marketing have multiplied despite the methodological difficulties associated with this area of research as well as problems concerning the definition, operationalization, measurement and classification of concepts within the extensive category of affect (Bagozzi et al., 1999). Marketing literature has shown how emotions and moods play a significant role in the cognitive processes of consumers, and how recognizing the relevance of the affective component impacts an enterprise's marketing choices at both the strategic and operational level.

Operational marketing has been heavily affected by studies into consumption emotions, especially with regard to the use of distribution, product and communication levers such as distribution policies based on 'experiential shopping' principles. Donovan and Rossiter (1982) demonstrate that the affective component is a determining factor in purchase decisions. In fact, while the cognitive component plays an important role in planned shopping, impulse purchases are influenced by the atmosphere of the sales outlet and the emotions it can arouse in consumers. With regard to the relationship between the affective component and product lever management, some authors (Hirschman and Holbrook, 1982; Batra and Athola, 1990; Mano and Oliver, 1993) have conceptualized the utilitarian and hedonic components of goods: the former refers to the functional attributes of the product, the latter to its aesthetic and emotional characteristics. The implications of this distinction are important, as it has been demonstrated that consumers employ a wide variety of product evaluation processes depending on which of the two components prevails, that is, whether the product can be attributed to *thinking* or *feeling*. As regards advertising, on the other hand, most studies of emotions focus on the problem of the 'contingency approach' (Holbrook, 1978), that is, whether to use rational or emotional appeals. In this context, the marketing literature considers it advisable to use the first type of appeal when *thinking* products are advertised, while the second type should preferably be employed for *feeling* products (Vaughn, 1980).

The study of the affective component of advertising also involves an analysis of the emotions aroused by the context, such as television programmes interrupted by commercials. For example, Goldberg and Gorn (1987) verify the existence of a relationship between types of television programmes and the effectiveness of the commercials 'hosted' by those programmes. The authors show that a commercial is more effective in terms of recollection and recognition when it 'interrupts' a comedy rather than a dramatic film. Moreover, Pavelchak et al. (1988) showed that the level of spectator involvement also impacts the effectiveness of advertisements inserted in the programme, as television commercials are rapidly forgotten when they are associated with broadcasts that might 'enchant' the audience.

Erevelles (1998) and Bagozzi et al. (1999) point out that it can be useful to analyse the emotional component in other areas of marketing, for example by addressing the role of emotions in strategic marketing. In the same vein, Aaker and Lee (2001) show that the emotions sought after by consumers during the moment of consumption can be a useful market segmentation criterion. It would also be helpful to study the merits of 'affective' versus 'cognitive' positioning. Another area of research would be the product life cycle; for example, in which stages of the life cycle is it most appropriate to stimulate the market with affective or rational appeals? Brand equity and brand extension are two additional streams of research that could benefit from an emotion-oriented approach to marketing. For example, given a particular product category, are *feeling* brands easier to extend than *thinking* ones? And if this hypothesis proved to be true, what implications might arise in terms of brand equity construction for brands with a prevailing emotional or rational component?

Psychological studies addressing the topic of emotions have also involved analytical marketing and consumer behaviour, which is the subject of this book. In particular, affective variables condition the analytical processes carried out by consumers when they absorb and process marketing stimuli, form their behaviours and systems of preferences, and ultimately make choices. In particular, some studies have investigated the impact of the affective component on the motivational system of consumers. For example, scholars have analysed the effects of various moods on how information is received (Keller et al., 2002) and remembered (Lee and Sternthal, 1999). It has also been demonstrated that the affective component involves the formation of behaviour (e.g., Howard and Gengler, 2001), choice processes (e.g., Garbarino and Edell, 1997; Otnes et al., 1997; Luce, 1998; Pham et al., 2001) and post-purchase behaviour (e.g., Tsiros and Mittal, 2000; Romani et al., 2012).[1] The studies cited examine various affective variables, not just emotions, and involve all stages of the purchasing and consumption process. However, this contribution will focus exclusively on consumption emotions, a choice that will be justified in the next section.

1.2 AFFECT AND EMOTIONS

Addressing the role played by emotions in the purchase and consumption process is a difficult task, not only because it involves exploring uncharted territory but also due to the complexity of the concept itself. According to Ben-Ze'ev (2000), this complexity can largely be attributed to three factors.

First of all, emotions appear to be extremely sensitive to personal and contextual factors. Therefore, an emotion might be felt in a certain situation but not in another identical situation because after the first time that situation has become 'familiar'. This characteristic of emotions is fundamentally important to the study of consumption phenomena. In fact, the dynamic nature of individual emotions requires enterprises to adopt an equally dynamic emotion management process, which, when competition is more intense, must even anticipate market expectations.

The second source of complexity is the fact that emotions are rarely experienced one at a time, as individuals often experience combinations of emotions. For example, love and joy are often accompanied by jealousy and fear of losing a loved one. Similarly, in the context of consumption, post-purchase behaviour differs because it originates from different combinations of emotions experienced during the moment of consumption and not from individual emotional phenomena. For example, dissatisfied customers who feel that the producer or service provider is at fault will experience dissatisfaction as well as a feeling of anger, which they will vent by making a complaint or by spreading negative word of mouth. On the other hand, customers who are dissatisfied because they consider themselves to be unfortunate, that is, they believe their dissatisfaction is due to adverse circumstances, will probably simply feel sad or sorry and will not behave negatively towards those who supplied the goods or services. The behaviour adopted by individuals in the post-consumption phase is significant for management because of its important implications in terms of service recovery and learning. Therefore, the combinations of emotions that help shape consumers' judgements of satisfaction/dissatisfaction constitute a highly important field of study.

The third cause underlying the complexity of emotive meaning is rooted in linguistic differences, which themselves reflect important cultural differences. These differences make it difficult for those who do not share the same cultural background to fully understand emotive phenomena. For example, the Italian language does not have a word for the German emotion *Schadenfreude*. It can only be translated with the locution 'pleasure from the misfortunes of others'. Similarly, it is difficult for an Italian to fully understand the *saudade*[2] emotion known in Portuguese culture. Such linguistic differences require thorough comprehension and analysis at both the managerial and academic level, especially among those responsible for international marketing.

The complexity of emotion means that it is both preferable and more common to use prototype categories rather than binary categories to describe the phenomenon (Elster, 1999; Ben-Ze'ev, 2000). Binary categories prescribe a net classification criterion, that is, one that defines the conditions required in order to belong to a certain class. In particular, these categories have two peculiarities: the existence of a rule that unambiguously establishes whether an element or item belongs to a class or not, and an equal degree of belonging among the items in a given category. For example, the state of pregnancy can be defined as a binary category: a woman is either expectant or she is not, and she cannot be 'somewhat pregnant'. Similarly, no woman can be 'more pregnant' than another.

In contrast, membership in a prototype category is determined by the degree of similarity between the element classified and the 'best representative of the category', or the 'typical case'. The more similar an element is to the typical case, the greater its degree of belonging to the category. The idea of a 'house', for example, is a prototype rather than a binary category. We can therefore say that both the concept of 'apartment' and that of 'carapace' can belong to the 'house' category, and that the former exhibits a higher degree of belonging to this category than the latter. Prototype categories seem particularly suitable for describing and classifying phenomena within the affective sphere, including emotions.

In this sense, 'typical emotion' is characterized by the following features: presence of a specific sensation, sudden and spontaneous appearance, brief duration, physiological activation, a particular facial expression, partiality, cognitive origin, and a tendency to act. As discussed in the brief analysis below, some of these features are extremely interesting for consumer behaviour analysis:

- *Presence of a specific sensation.* According to Elster (1999), when individuals experience any kind of emotion they have the impression that it stands for a particular sensation; just like when one perceives a colour, it seems that an emotion can be identified and recognized for specific quality characteristics, such as tonality or intensity.
- *Sudden and spontaneous appearance.* The sudden appearance of emotions has a fundamental adaptive value: emotions allow individuals to address situations without wasting time.[3] In fact, both apathy and an excess of rationality can be a waste of time, which might compromise the satisfaction of personal

objectives in many cases. Emotions arise when individuals perceive that their objectives and interests are promoted or potentially thwarted by events (Oatley, 1992). In the former case, subjects experience positive emotions, while in the latter case the emotions are negative. Consumers who suffer a disservice and realize they have been swindled will react with an immediate complaint only when they experience anger. In such cases, negative emotions can allow them to 'stand up for their rights' and therefore not compromise their financial situations or their general well-being. Indifference or a complex rationalization of the event could prove less efficient for the satisfaction of their needs as consumers. Again, with reference to the example of swindled customers, the emotion of anger arises spontaneously in that it is not sought after or desired by the customer.

- *Brief duration.* Consumers experience an emotion for a short time: in the example above, as soon as they vent their anger the feeling of discomfort goes away and does not accompany them for the rest of the day. Brevity of duration is one of the main distinctions between emotions and moods, with the former being short and the latter being long in duration.
- *Physiological activation and facial expressions.* The service provider will have probably seen anger in the facial expressions of the consumer and in characteristic physiological activations – such as flushing in the face – even before the protest is expressed verbally.
- *Partiality.* The characteristic of partiality refers to the fact that emotions are elicited by particular events and not by general situations: it is difficult for individuals to get angry at the thought of potential swindles by shopkeepers, but people are disturbed by specific situations that involve them directly. Corporate communication managers know perfectly well that in order to involve recipients emotionally, it is necessary to make reference to specific cases and not to general ones in order to assimilate the context of the message into the target audience's experience and thus into its cognitive or emotive schemata. Like duration, partiality also makes it possible to distinguish emotion from mood, which is defined by contrast 'as the experience of global situational meaning structures' (Frijda, 1986, p. 252). In fact, moods do not appear to be con-

nected to specific situations: for example, unlike emotions such as fear or anger, it is often more difficult to trace the root cause of a good or bad mood.

- *Cognitive origin.* Emotions have a *cognitive origin* in the sense that they derive from an appraisal of present, past or, in the case of anticipated emotions (see Box 1.1), future events. In the case in point, the cognitive origin of anger lies in the fact that consumers believe they have been wronged. Cognitive psychology highlights the fact that every emotion derives not from the triggering event, but from the individual's evaluation of that event: consumers feel anger not for the disservice in itself, but because they consider the disservice to be the provider's fault.

- *Tendency to act.* Lastly, emotions also involve a tendency to act, that is, an impulse to take real and proper action rather than to inhibit action. In the example above, complaints and negative word of mouth are two actions that can arise from the anger of the swindled consumer.

If typical emotions are characterized by the features listed above, then we can accept the definition of emotions that was put forth by Bagozzi et al. (2002) and incorporates those features. According to those authors, emotion is 'a mental state of readiness that arises from cognitive appraisals,[4] has a phenomenological tone, is accompanied by physiological processes and may result in specific actions' (Bagozzi et al., 2002, p. 37).

Now that a definition of emotion has been proposed and the concept has been distinguished from mood, it is necessary to define a number of terms associated with the affective sphere. Unlike emotions, these concepts are not the subject of this book, but they do appear in the discussion below. *Affect*, a word that has already been mentioned extensively in this chapter, is an umbrella term, a general concept concerning the quality and central features of the emotive experience and that attributes to the latter its non-cognitive nature.

In contrast, *feeling* refers to an affective mindset directed towards a specific object in a relatively stable way. Such a mindset is produced on the basis of previous experiences or through social learning. Like emotions (but unlike moods), sentiments focus on a specific object, but unlike emotions (and like moods) they also exhibit a certain temporal stability.

BOX 1.1 ANTICIPATED EMOTIONS

An interesting study by Bagozzi et al. (1998) suggests that the emotive experience can play a crucial role not only during the consumption process or in post-purchase behaviour, but also before purchasing or subscribing to a service, that is, when customers plan their financial actions with a view to reaching an objective.

Although they propose a generic model for the analysis of behaviour aimed at reaching an objective and not specifically for the study of consumer behaviour, the authors consider it reasonable to suppose that anticipated attitudes and emotions can also affect purchase behaviour.

More precisely, the three authors studied the behaviour of a sample of individuals who had set out to maintain (or reach) their proper body weight. The scholars investigated the role played by positive and negative anticipated emotions in achieving this objective. Individuals who adhere to a diet and do physical exercise in order to reach or maintain a certain weight are also encouraged to make these sacrifices by the emotions that arise when they visualize themselves as physically fit (positive anticipated emotion), or by those that arise when they imagine failing to achieve the established goal and the resulting future situation of discomfort (negative anticipated emotion). More precisely, positive emotions experienced by individuals when they imagine reaching perfect physical form may include feelings of satisfaction, happiness, pride, self-assurance, and so on. On the other hand, imagining failure can arouse negative emotions such as anger, frustration, guilt, shame, and so forth. Scholars have demonstrated that this type of emotion plays a central role in the pursuit of an objective.

Lastly, the term *temperament* defines the set of individual features and differences, seen as relatively coherent fundamental behavioural tendencies, present early on in life, strongly affected by biological factors, concerning the manifestation of emotiveness, activity, reactivity and sociability. This is a narrower concept compared to *personality*, which includes cognitive structures such as a person's concept of self, system of values, expectations, and so on, and broader compared to the *emotive trait*, which refers to purely emotive dimensions.

Among the various characteristics that distinguish emotions from other concepts related to the affective sphere, the cognitive origin and action tendency are clearly very important for marketing activities. By implementing suitable marketing policies designed to influence the appraisal of cognitive antecedents, company management can direct the affective processes individuals undergo in the consumption experience and therefore guide their post-purchase attitudes and behaviour. Even if the literature concerning consumer behaviour has examined all of the affective variables introduced above, the managerial implications of studies on consumption emotion appear to be of greater interest. For this reason, consumer emotions are the main subject of this book and for the same reason it may be interesting, from a managerial point of view, to focus our attention on the cognitive antecedents of emotions.

1.3 EMOTIONS: COGNITIVE ANTECEDENTS

According to the cognitive theory of emotions, cognitive antecedents are the quintessence of emotion and make it possible to distinguish this concept from the other variables involved in the affective sphere. In this regard, the cognitive point of view states that 'the experience of emotion is closely associated with the organism's appraisal of its environment along several cognitive dimensions' (Smith and Ellsworth, 1985, p. 817) and that emotions differ depending on individual appraisals of a certain occurrence. Appraisal is a particular type of cognitive activity, which consists in 'a continuing evaluation of the significance of what is happening for one's personal well-being' (Lazarus, 1991, p. 144). Lazarus (1991) therefore highlights an important difference between knowledge and appraisal: the former may not concern individual well-being, and it does not necessarily have personal meaning. Appraisal can be a type of automatic assessment of which we are not necessarily aware (Lazarus, 1982). Therefore, various emotions are not simply elicited by the event itself, but rather by the individual's interpretation of the event (Ortony et al.,

1988). Different appraisals of the same event can trigger different emotions.

Naturally, individual differences affect the cognitive processing of a certain stimulus, but I do not regard them as an obstacle to the construction of a theory on consumption emotions. In fact, it can be reasonably assumed that different individuals belonging to the same cultural context will experience similar emotions in response to the same events (Averill, 1982).

The psychological literature concerning appraisal is fairly extensive (Smith and Ellsworth, 1985; Weiner, 1985; Frijda, 1986, 1987, 1993; Ortony et al., 1988; Lazarus, 1991; Roseman, 1991; Scherer, 1993) and exhibits a certain degree of convergence (Scherer, 1988). Given the focus on consumer behaviour, I will focus on the most important ones with regard to purchase and consumption processes and the distinction of the different consumption emotions I will analyse in the following: the *desirability* and the *causation* of an event.

In the first type of appraisal, the subject assesses whether a certain situation can promote or obstruct the pursuit of a certain objective (Scherer, 1988). The importance of this antecedent has been highlighted by Lazarus (1991), who defines this appraisal as 'goal congruence/incongruence', an evaluation that considers 'the extent to which a transaction is consistent or inconsistent with what the person wants – that is, it either thwarts or facilitates personal goals' (Lazarus, 1991, p. 150). Appraisal has been referred to as 'goal/ path obstacle' (Smith and Ellsworth, 1985), 'desirability' (Ortony et al., 1988) and 'motive consistency' (Roseman, 1991). This type of appraisal generally arouses emotions from the areas of pleasure and regret (Ortony et al., 1988) and makes it possible to distinguish positive emotions from negative ones (Weiner, 1985).

The objectives pursued by individuals can concern their own well-being or that of their loved ones. When an event is perceived as relevant to the well-being of other people, this type of consideration produces empathetic emotions, such as compassion; on the other hand, when the pursued objective has personal relevance, appraisals elicit egocentric emotions, such as pride (Scherer, 1988) as I will analyse in Chapter 3.

The goals of individuals can be further classified as interests concerning one's person (e.g., survival), one's relationships (e.g., belonging to a group) or the social dimension in the broadest sense of the term (e.g., social respectability). The objectives included in the third category are often motivated by the specific values and rules of a given social context. For example, honour, deference towards one's superiors and control of one's emotive expressions are existential aims in certain cultures, but not in others (Frijda, 1986). Scherer (1988) demonstrates that appraisals related to the pursuit of (or failure to achieve) these three types of goals bring about different emotions.

Furthermore, the level of desirability associated with success must be related to the importance an individual attributes to that success (Ortony et al., 1988). This, in turn, can be rooted in the central rather than the peripheral collocation of that particular goal in the pursuit of individual existential objectives (Ortony et al., 1988; Scherer, 1988; Lazarus, 1991). For example, a good result in a university exam can fill students with pride and happiness if they consider that success crucial to their professional careers (existential objective), or it can elicit less intense emotions if the positive result is assigned a peripheral role in the pursuit of this existential objective. The central or peripheral dimension of achieving or failing to achieve a certain goal determines the intensity of the positive and negative emotions aroused.

Finally, according to a classification suggested by Frijda (1986), interests can either be manifest or latent in the sense that 'interests are mainly dormant demons' (Frijda, 1986, p. 456). This distinction is also important for predicting the intensity of the emotions experienced by an individual. An objective is manifest in cases where the subject is aware of its existence and undertakes plans to pursue it. On the other hand, an interest is latent when it is unconscious: the subject only becomes aware of it when she experiences the positive or negative emotions that indicate whether or not it has been achieved. In this case, therefore, emotions 'can arrive like thieves in the night, the night being the dormant demon' (ibid., p. 458). One example is a sudden yearning for a love that one supposed was forgotten but is in fact still alive (ibid.). Therefore, emotions arise both when events promote or obstruct manifest interests and when they correspond to or oppose latent interests. Thus the distinction between the two typologies 'is not essential with respect to the arising of emotions, if one excludes the fact that active interests are associated with stronger expectations, with the consequence that this has on the intensity of the emotion' (ibid.).

A second type of appraisal that is undoubtedly important for marketing studies relates to the causation of an event: when a subject examines an event, she can feel responsible for it, or attribute responsibility to other people or other circumstances (Scherer, 1988). Agency (Smith and Ellsworth, 1985; Roseman, 1991) and locus (Weiner, 1985) are two alternative ways of expressing appraisal. This is a type of universal evaluation by individuals belonging to all cultures and generations, and it is characterized by an important adaptive value. For these reasons, the theory of emotion and motivation is based on causation (Weiner, 1985). When individuals attribute their successes or failures to circumstances, they will feel happy or sad; on the other hand, if they accept personal responsibility for them or attribute them to other people, they will experience emotions connected with judgements of approval or disapproval (Ortony et al., 1988). With reference to this type of appraisal, Scherer (1988) notes that the search for a person responsible for a certain event is frequently accompanied by an investigation into the motives of the parties responsible and reveals that it is precisely the reasoning behind those motives that elicit specific emotions: if someone hits us, we will react in totally different ways depending on whether they did so intentionally or unintentionally (ibid.). Weiner (1985) defines this aspect of causation as controllability: a negative or positive outcome can be caused intentionally or unintentionally. This is an important aspect because it allows us to predict the precise emotions experienced by an individual. As Weiner aptly puts it, when faced with failure we get angry with lazy people but not with incompetent ones, with whom we tend to sympathize instead (Weiner, 1985, p. 562).

As assumed below and demonstrated in Chapter 5, the different possible combinations of these two appraisals elicit different consumption emotions capable of predicting different post-purchase actions, such as complaints, repurchase or word of mouth. An analysis of these two cognitive antecedents is relevant because it may allow managers to anticipate the behaviour of consumers and, hypothetically, to influence their appraisal of the consumption experience by taking suitable marketing actions.

Some interesting criticisms have been levelled at the appraisal theory. These objections can be summarized in the following three questions (Roseman and Smith, 2001). Do appraisals really cause emotions, or are they rather a component, if not a consequence, of the emotive response? Are appraisals a necessary condition of emotions or can emotions arise regardless of appraisals? Are appraisals a sufficient cause for emotions?

As regards the first question, we have underlined the fact that appraisal theory defines appraisals as antecedents of emotions. For example, when consumers are swindled and become aware of the damage they have suffered, they will probably be angry with the provider who swindled them. We can also presume that these consumers will vent their anger through negative word of mouth, and when reporting the event, they may also remember other wrongs done to them by the same provider or by the same category of providers. This anger can therefore elicit additional reflections that may further exacerbate the consumer's discomfort. This example highlights how appraisals can also derive from emotions. On the other hand, numerous studies mentioned in this book are based on experiments that involve the manipulation of cognitive antecedents, and those research efforts have demonstrated that different combinations of appraisals are able to elicit different emotive states. In conclusion, this cognitive dimension can both precede and follow an emotive experience.

The second question was answered in a complex study by Izard (1993), which shows that emotions can be elicited by neural processes (e.g., endogenously by hormones and exogenously by pharmacological agents), by motivational processes (such as hunger and thirst) and by cognitive processes (i.e., appraisals). Furthermore, any readers who have overindulged in alcohol at least once in their lives know perfectly well that Izard's assumptions are more than plausible and that the answer to the first part of the question is certainly negative. However, especially in connection with consumption emotions, it is also true that emotions are rarely arbitrary reactions disconnected from reasoning on events concerning our existence. For this reason, appraisals are considered an important element of consumer behaviour analysis even though they are not a necessary condition for emotions.

Finally, responding to the last point requires us to address the following questions. Is it possible to perceive danger without experiencing fear? Or, can we be swindled without being assailed by a feeling of anger? This can happen because emotions arise more from multiple reasoning, a combination of antecedents rather than from a specific antecedent. Therefore, this consideration can very well justify why a consumer who is afraid of flying would react calmly to the sudden cancellation of a flight.

1.4 EMOTIONS: ACTION TENDENCIES

In line with the cognitive theory, emotions, once elicited, prepare people to cope with a certain situation in an adaptive way: together with appraisals, coping is an essential part of the emotive process (Lazarus, 1991). Psychologists have attempted to identify and classify the different coping strategies implemented by people in order to address certain events (e.g., Folkman et al., 1986; Carver et al., 1989; Skinner et al., 2003). For the sake of illustration, Table 1.1 shows one of the most frequently mentioned classifications of strategies implemented to cope with unfavourable events.

The concept of coping is similar to the action tendency proposed by Frijda (1986), that is, a state of readiness to perform a certain type of action. In Frijda's theorization of the emotive experience, the concept of action tendency becomes so relevant as to define the

Table 1.1   Coping methods

Coping item	Possible instances
Confrontive coping	The individual fights for what he or she wants, tries to win over people who obstruct him or her and gets angry with the people who created the problem
Distancing	The individual refuses to take the situation too seriously
Self-control	The person does not express his or her emotions and tries to conceal the seriousness of the situation from other people
Seeking social support	The person seeks concrete help or asks friends and acquaintances for advice
Accepting responsibility	The person realizes he or she is the main cause of his or her problems and promises to behave differently in future
Escape/avoidance	The person hopes that the problem will miraculously solve itself on its own
Planful problem solving	The individual draws up an action plan to address the problem
Positive reappraisal	The subject attempts to find positive aspects in an unfavourable situation

Source: Adapted from Lazarus (1999, p. 115).

very concept of emotion itself: 'Emotions then can be defined as modes of relational action readiness, either in the form of tendencies to establish, maintain, or disrupt a relationship with the environment or in the form of mode of relational readiness as such' (Frijda, 1986, p.119). These can be concrete physical actions, such as escape, attack or insult; or also purely cognitive actions, such as thinking continuously of a person when one is deeply in love (Frijda, 1986). In the same way that combinations of different appraisals elicit specific emotive states, it can be said that different action tendencies correspond to different emotions (ibid.). For example, anger implies an impulse to attack, fear implies escape from threatening events, and so on. As defined by Frijda, action readiness does not necessarily prepare the subject to perform an evident action: there are different levels of readiness. The subject can be ready to act or simply prepare several action plans that can be carried out at a later stage if the circumstances are conducive to one of these strategies; or she can attempt to interrupt the cognitive processes that distract her from solving an urgent problem. Like scholars who study coping strategies, Frijda (1986) and Frijda et al. (1989) also suggest a classification of action readiness methods and maintain that positive emotions also elicit precise behavioural responses (Table 1.2).

As discussed further below, the concepts of coping and action tendency can be of great interest to marketing scholars. In fact, we will see how customers' post-purchase behaviour, such as repurchase, complaints or word of mouth, can be considered behavioural responses triggered by specific emotions, which themselves are elicited by particular combinations of appraisals, that is, individual assessments of the consumption experience. Therefore, if management is able to understand and react to the consumer appraisal process, it will also be able to guide post-purchase behaviour that is useful or harmful to the enterprise (Yi and Baumgartner, 2004).

1.5   CLASSES OF EMOTIONS

In section 1.3 we examined how certain combinations of appraisals can elicit specific emotions, while in the previous section we correlated individual emotive experiences with certain action tendencies. On the other hand, as highlighted in the second paragraph of section 1.4, emotions are experienced in combination. In this regard, it is

Table 1.2   Action readiness methods

Action readiness items	Forms
Approach	Desiring to approach, to be near or close
Be with	Wishing to be with a person
Protection	Desiring to be protected from someone or something
Avoidance	Desiring to keep away from a situation
Attending	Wishing to see, understand, pay attention
Distance	Wishing to keep someone or something away
Rejection	Wishing to have nothing to do with someone or something
Disinterest	Not paying attention to anything that might be going on
Don't want	Wishing for a different situation, wishing that something had not happened
Boiling inwardly	Fuming inside
Antagonistic	Wanting to oppose, attack, harm or insult
Reaction	Wanting to overcome an obstacle, to conquer
Interruption	Interrupting something or being interrupted
Distraction	Being unable to concentrate or think clearly
In command	Being in control of the situation; knowing what to do
Help	Wishing to help someone, take care of someone
Disappear from view	Wishing to hide, not to be noticed
Inhibition	Being frozen, paralysed
Blushing	Blushing; fear of blushing
Submitting	Not opposing; submitting to the desire of others
Apathy	Not interested in anything
Giving up	Giving up, forgetting about it
Shutting off	Withdrawing into oneself
Helplessness	Desiring to do something, but not knowing what to do; feeling powerless
Crying	Crying or feeling the impulse to cry
Excitement	Feeling the urge to move all the time
Exuberance	Desiring to do something, jump, sing
Laughing	Laughing or feeling the impulse to laugh
Rest	Feeling calm and at rest

Source: Adapted from Frijda et al. (1989, p.214).

important to note that consumer behaviour studies that include the affective variable do not necessarily examine the behavioural effects of discrete emotions, but sometimes investigate the implications of classes of emotions (e.g., Hosany and Prayag, 2011).

There are various reference models for identifying classes of emotions. In fact, psychologists have drawn up a large number of classifications. Together with Plutchik (1962), Izard (1977) was one of the first authors to propose a classification of emotions, which comprised a model of ten fundamental emotions: interest, enjoyment, surprise, sadness, anger, disgust, happiness, fear, shame and guilt. For his part, Plutchik (1962) maintains that emotions can either be primary or mixed. The first type represents emotions connected with the basic behaviour necessary for the survival of the human species. These emotions include joy, anger, fear, disgust, contempt, surprise and sadness. Mixed emotions, on the other hand, arise from a combination of two or more primary emotions in different proportions. A study by Shaver et al. (1987) classifies 135 moods that can be called emotions and are based on six macro-factors: love, happiness, surprise, anger, unhappiness and fear.

Mehrabian and Russell (1974) developed a classification of emotions that is widely used in marketing studies, especially retailing. Their PAD model traces all emotions back to three factors: *pleasure*, including all the moods connected with pleasure or displeasure, such as joy and sadness; *arousal*, including emotions connected with states of excitement or apathy, such as boredom or surprise; and *dominance*, which refers to emotions involving the sensation of control or loss of control over a situation (e.g., fear and worry). For example, a sales outlet might be designed to arouse these three classes of emotions in visitors: suitably designed category management can use dominance by helping customers to identify the products on their shopping lists; a creatively designed shop window can have an impact on pleasure, while promotional activities featuring a product test, for example, might increase arousal. In a simpler classification based on desirability appraisal, emotions can also be categorized as positive (generated by favourable events) or negative (generated by unfavourable events).

Arousal and desirability are fundamental components in the papers published by Mano and Oliver (1993) and Hirschman and Stern (1999). Both studies identify affect as a two-dimensional construct that can be classified with reference to arousal and positive

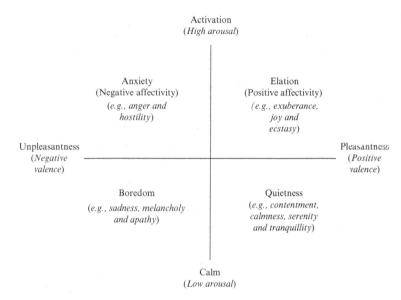

Source: Adapted from Mano and Oliver (1993) and Hirschman and Stern (1999).

Figure 1.1   Classification of emotions based on arousal and desirability

value. In fact, as stated by Mano and Oliver (1993, p. 463), if desirability lies at the basis of the consumption experience, arousal undoubtedly defines the tone of the consumer's emotive state. By crossing the two variables of arousal and pleasure as shown in Figure 1.1, we obtain four quadrants that depict the different characteristics of consumers' potential emotive responses.

On the other hand, O'Shaughnessy and O'Shaughnessy (2003) categorized emotions as factive and epistemic: while the former are generated by a conscious or unconscious analysis of an event, the latter emerge from considerations concerning the probability that an event will occur. Factive emotions include joy, embarrassment and shame. Marketing actions can set out to inhibit or emphasize these types of emotions; for example, the 'Stop sweat' headline proposed by an advertising agency to promote a deodorant elicits the emotion of embarrassment arising from failure to use the product. In contrast, emotions such as fear or hope are classified as epistemic. These are very important emotions for marketing managers: cosmetics advertising, for example, is often designed to arouse hopes in potential purchasers, while public service campaigns make frequent use of fear appeals to promote responsible behaviour.

Purchase and consumption moments can be favourable or unfavourable events that are capable of generating emotions. To a certain extent, consumers can experience the emotions that arise from using a product before the purchase phase or after the consumption phase, as discussed below. In this sense, it is rather restrictive to use the term 'stimulus' to describe the element that activates an emotion given the fact that appraisal activities can involve the consumer's imagination, fantasy and recollection.

With regard to the possible classes of emotions and the approach followed in this book, we will refer to the appraisals of causation in order to classify the different cluster of emotions. Namely, the consumption emotions described in the second chapter are roughly based on circumstances, the ones presented in the third chapter on the self, while anger and gratitude are elicited by the product/service provider.

If we acknowledge the possibility that certain appraisal combinations can generate emotions, we can attempt to study this variable as a discrete phenomenon. This point of view is of particular interest to scholars of consumer behaviour because when a single emotion is predictive of precise post-purchase behaviour, it is useful to analyse its distinctive elements as well as examine the aggregates of emotive states.

1.6 CONSUMER EMOTIONS AND BEHAVIOUR

Especially with regard to the cognitive processes of consumers, psychology and marketing research has examined the influence of the affective sphere on the decisions taken by consumers. It has been demonstrated that emotional states affect various phases of the purchase and consumption process. In this sense, we can identify four phases: the pre-purchase experience, purchase, consumption and the post-purchase experience:

- *The pre-purchase experience.* The study by Bagozzi et al. (1998) mentioned in Box 1.1 suggests how emotive experience can play a role in the pre-purchase phase. For example, let us examine the purchase of a luxury item such as an engagement ring. Buyers may be induced to experience a sense of guilt when they prepare to commit considerable financial resources to a precious – but in a certain sense useless – object. These are what we refer to as 'anticipated emotions', that is, emotions experienced by consumers when they plan their financial actions in order to achieve an objective. The management of negative anticipated emotions is clearly a critical issue in the luxury goods sector, which frequently carries out marketing activities designed to reduce these emotions. This is the precise intention of the text used in the Zales Diamonds global advertising campaign: communicating directly with the future groom, the headline provocatively asks whether a gift for one's lifelong companion is perhaps not worth two months' salary. Emotions not only condition behaviour, but also the phase in which product information is collected, as consumers store that information in memory and assess choice alternatives. For example, it has been shown that a positive mindset encourages the recovery of positive recollections (Isen et al., 1978) and that the affective intensity, that is, a high level of emotive involvement, conditions recollection processes: brands featuring a dominant affective component are more readily recalled than those that stand out largely for their cognitive features.

- *The purchase experience.* As analysed in the chapters that follow, the purchase experience itself can be influenced by affective elements. The use of specific payment methods, the selection of a certain distribution channel, or a meeting with the provider can be opportunities for experiencing emotions.
- *The consumption experience.* Naturally, strong emotions such as pleasure and gratification will have the greatest potential effect on the consumption experience. These are positive emotions that can be amplified by marketing managers, for example by designing and adding value to a community dimension of consumption. One example can be found in Ducati's management of real and virtual communities of bikers who own that particular brand. Ducati biker meetings fill the brand experience with emotion: the sense of belonging that unites individuals who share the same interest or passion gives the focal product or activity an aura of 'sacredness' (Celsi et al., 1993).

● *The post-consumption experience.* Lastly, emotions can also arise after the moment of consumption. For example, historical imagination and fantastic imagination (Hirschman and Holbrook, 1982) arouse the emotions of consumption in the minds of consumers. In the case of historical imagination, consumers recollect the consumption experience; in fantastic imagination, consumers look forward to the pleasure of a consumption event they have never experienced before. Therefore, if it is true that the use of a product can arouse strong emotions, it can be plausibly assumed that they do not simply terminate upon consumption. Moreover, as discussed in the next chapter, studies into the nostalgic vein of consumption that have analysed the impact of historical imagination in the last ten years clearly show that emotions connected with products that were popular during a particular phase of an individual's life have an enduring effect on her consumption behaviour. The phenomenon of nostalgia has been studied widely, not only in relation to the consumption of leisure products such as music and films, but also in the context of more functional products such as cars. Recollections of products consumed at specific ages (e.g., the reference age group for music consumption is around 23.5 years old) are also preferred for a long time afterwards. The emotions associated with the experience of consuming those products can therefore extend this experience for a far longer time, even for a lifetime.

1.7 CONSUMPTION EMOTIONS: A PREDICTIVE MODEL OF POST-PURCHASE BEHAVIOUR BASED ON EMOTIONS

As mentioned above, this book mainly focuses on one of the affective variables mentioned in section 1.2, namely emotions, and the empirical research presented above. In this context, predictions of post-purchase behaviour are based on the consumption phase. The model in question is outlined in Figure 1.2.

As the model shows, it is assumed that particular combinations of causation and desirability appraisals (as discussed in section 1.3) generate specific emotions in consumers when they consume a product. In turn, these emotions then generate specific action

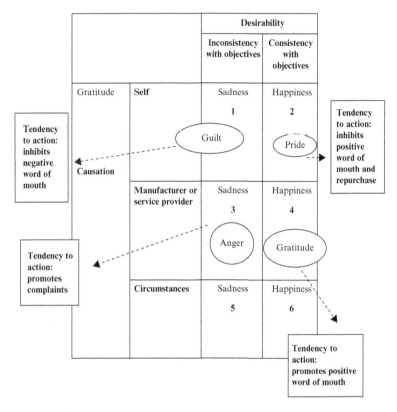

Figure 1.2   Consumption emotions: cognitive antecedents and action tendencies

tendencies. For example, an investor who purchased Icelandic bonds before the country defaulted can only feel angry with the financial consultant who recommended the purchase if the investor decided to put full faith in the consultant or if the latter played down the risks of the investment. Such a purchase experience can therefore be placed in box 3 of the matrix shown in Figure 1.2.

In this case, in fact, the investor's earnings expectations were frustrated due to the imprudent advice of the consultant. The anger deriving from a consumption experience of this type may generate a complaint as a action tendency. On the other hand, the consumer might feel guilty if she knowingly took the risk, thus compromising the family's finances in pursuit of easy earnings. This experience would be assigned to box 1 of the matrix and can generate regret as well as a feeling of guilt, which would inhibit complaints regarding the institution promoting the investment or regarding the Icelandic government.

The fifth chapter presents an empirical verification of the model in question. This framework is based on some of the psychological concepts presented above: appraisal, emotion and action tendency. In order to fully understand the distinctive characteristics of the six emotions presented in the figure as well as their cognitive origins, their relevant management implications and similar affective states, we will later analyse these concepts using both psychological and managerial approaches. In particular, Chapter 2 will examine the cognitive antecedents and action tendencies linked to happiness and unhappiness. Chapter 3 is devoted to an analysis of what are known as social emotions, in particular guilt and pride. These are affective feelings that pervade consumers' lives and have important consequences for the production and marketing of goods and services. Chapter 4 addresses anger and gratitude, emotional states that customers experience when they attribute full responsibility for a happy or unhappy consumption experience to the producer or service provider. In such cases, management also has tools at its disposal to prevent or generate these affective dimensions and to manage them when they are experienced by customers.

NOTES

1. For an exhaustive review of the influence of affective variables on purchase and consumption processes, see Bagozzi et al. (2002).
2. The feeling of longing for someone or something that you love and is lost. Or even a vague and constant desire for something that does not and probably cannot exist.
3. The analysis of consumer emotions that I propose clearly adopts the functionalist point of view, in which 'emotions do something and, presumably, they do it well; they are functional to the satisfaction of interests and they do so by controlling the level of importance of events and modulating or instigating action in a congruent way' (Frijda, 1986, p.635). Obviously, this point of view cannot be demonstrated: it is a point of view, a 'presumption' (Frijda, 1986).
4. Given the proposed definition of emotion and the objective of setting cognitive theory against behavioural theory, this book relies on a cognitive approach to the analysis of consumption emotion. Even if cognitive theory is currently the dominant paradigm as regards the elicitation of emotions, other psychological theories (such as behavioural theory) maintain that the conscious or unconscious analysis of a stimulus is not a necessary condition for an emotion to arise. Zajonc,

a psychologist and exponent of this school, expresses his scepticism about the cognitive position by taking the formation of electoral preferences as an example. If a voter says he or she is proud to vote for candidate A due to the latter's honesty, we can think of several ways of inducing him or her to be ashamed of his or her choice. For example, we can provide the voter with proof that candidate A is dishonest. However, as Zajonc maintains, '[t]he possibilities of success of this strategy are equal to those implemented to persuade a child who hates spinach to love it' (Zajonc, 1980, p. 159).

2. Happiness and unhappiness

This chapter is dedicated to what are known as individual emotions. After analysing the cognitive antecedents and tendencies to action associated with happiness from a purely psychological point of view, we will discuss the role this emotion plays in the purchase and consumption process in the second section. In the subsequent sections, we will examine the emotions that belong to the same affective class: *satisfaction* can be considered a variant of happiness with low *arousal*, while *hope* can anticipate a state of joy and *fear* a state of sadness. Lastly, *nostalgia* comprises both pleasant and sad sensations, thus sharing both the cognitive antecedents of happiness and unhappiness. We will then analyse the managerial implications of all these emotive variants.

2.1 HAPPINESS AND UNHAPPINESS: COGNITIVE ANTECEDENTS AND TENDENCIES TO ACTION

The pursuit of happiness is a pipe dream of Western society; the American Declaration of Independence even considers it to be an inalienable right. In 2012, UK Prime Minister David Cameron launched a £2 million online survey in order to measure the level of happiness among UK citizens. According to Mr Cameron, the well-being of citizens should not only measured by GDP, but by an index that accounts for other factors such as life, marital and job satisfaction, satisfaction with income, perceived neighbourhood safety, and trust in politics. Given the importance of the issue, a master course in happiness was developed in Sardinia where professors aim to teach the art of joy. While these initiatives and the vast shelf space many bookshops devote to manuals on how to be happy may make us smile, we as marketing scholars must conduct a serious analysis of the reasons for these clamorous editorial successes. But what really makes us happy or sad?

Happiness (or joy)[1] and unhappiness are respectively interpreted in psychological literature as emotive responses to positive or negative events (Bagozzi, 1999). In particular, according to cognitive theories, relevance and desirability discussed in Chapter 1 are the two antecedents of these emotions (Izard, 1993; Lazarus, 1991).

Therefore, according to cognitive psychologists, when we assess an event that we consider significant and we believe it has produced a positive result with respect to the achievement of an objective, we feel happy. In particular, Oatley (1992) suggests a classification of these positive events, arguing that we experience the emotion of happiness when we manage to pursue an objective, when we see progress in a plan drawn up to achieve a result, when we obtain positive intermediate results, or even when we consider success to be very probable. For example, with reference to this classification, a scholar is happy when she manages to publish a research project in a prestigious journal (achieving an objective) or, even earlier, when the empirical data collected add value to her theories (progress in the plan), when her research stimulates interest and debate in the academic community (achieving an intermediate objective), or when she obtains substantially positive reviews (high probability of success).

As regards the antecedent of causality examined in Chapter 1, the debate in the literature is still open in this regard. According to Roseman (1991), circumstances are responsible for happiness. When, on the other hand, we mainly attribute success to ourselves, we feel proud,[2] while we feel sympathy or gratitude when we feel we are indebted to other people.[3] Oatley (1992) also notes that chance can elicit happiness, but it may also give rise to personal commitment or a combination of these two factors, as illustrated in the previous example. Lastly, Lazarus (1991) argues that the *appraisal* of causation does not play a significant role in connection with happiness, asserting that we feel happy following a positive event regardless of any judgement of responsibility for the outcome.

With reference to future expectations, psychological literature points out that happiness is the outcome of a *certain* positive result. On the other hand, when a situation is evolving favourably without having produced any security, the emotion experienced is *hope* rather than happiness. For example, an ill person who decides to follow a particular medical treatment programme in order to get well will be hopeful when she starts but will only be happy once she fully recovers. Hope, like joy, also has interesting marketing implications, as will be examined in section 2.3.

Happiness can focus on two substantial objects: it can lie in individual activities or in relationships with others (Bagozzi, 1999). With regard to relationships, psychological literature asserts that happiness is fundamentally an interpersonal emotion (Izard, 1991). Reciprocal understanding, a relationship based on affection, or the realization of a joint project typically bring about joyful moments. Concerning this point, Oatley (1992) cites descriptive research conducted in the United States at the end of the 1970s that indicates that Americans do not associate happiness with money, youth, power or health, but rather with marriage based on love. The relationship between these two emotions – love and happiness – is extremely complex,[4] and in this sense scholars define love as the interpersonal dimension of a state of happiness. Naturally, friendship can also be a source of happiness: Durkheim's cross-cultural study on suicide[5] demonstrates that people who have a lower sense of belonging to society, those who do not have close associations to specific reference groups and who do not experience social obligations are more inclined to take their lives than socially inserted individuals. It therefore appears that lonely people are often unhappy and that unhappy people are often lonely. A recent study conducted in the USA provides specific support for this conclusion by showing that the most glorious moments of the day comprise out-of-work socializing and sexual activities, both of which are typically relational experiences. Moreover, not only do we derive joy from relations with other people, but we also find happiness in dedicating ourselves to others. An interesting experiment by Lyubomirsky et al. (2005) demonstrates that constant commitment to charitable or simply kind actions, such as offering to take a friend to the airport, has a positive effect on personal well-being.

Happiness can derive from the activity itself rather than the achievement of an objective, and in particular from the individual activity of immersion in a creative process (Oatley, 1992). We feel happy when we engage in fulfilling activities in which we can fully express ourselves and that do not necessarily have to be brilliant productions. The performance of a choreography for a dancer, the preparation of a delicious dish for a gourmet, the writing of a book or the performance of a piece of music can be happy moments for people who perform those activities. Csikszentmihalyi (1990) defined this state of total immersion accompanying the creative process as *flow*, the expression of a talent rather than the execution of a challenging task. In this sense, happiness can be considered the first consequence of this state of immersion.

But is it *functional* to be happy? What tendencies to action are connected with joy? It is not easy to assign a precise function to joy (Lazarus, 1991), partly because positive emotions have generally been neglected by psychological studies (Tugade and Fredrickson, 2002). According to Oatley (1992), happiness is an emotion that tells us we have obtained a positive intermediate result. It therefore induces us to increase our dedication to achieving a final objective that we consider relevant. For example, once a person who has decided to lose weight sees that she has lost the first few pounds, she will joyfully note that her efforts have been rewarded and will follow a diet with increased rigour. It also seems that happiness performs an important social function. In fact, compared to sad people, happy people are more altruistic, more empathetic[6] and less diffident (Tugade and Fredrickson, 2002). This open attitude allows them to strengthen social ties, thus enriching their affective and relational culture. Therefore, as Tugade and Fredrickson (ibid., p.335) point out, 'positive emotions build personal and social resources to help individuals achieve better lives in the future'.

On the other hand, unhappiness derives from the ascertainment of a failure. As in the case of joy, the appraisals that appear to determine this emotion are relevance and desirability. Weiner (1985) deems the antecedent of causation to be irrelevant in this context: according to the author, joy and unhappiness are *attribution-independent* emotions in the sense that they are exclusively determined by the awareness of a success or a failure. Other scholars, such as Smith and Ellsworth (1985) and Roseman (1991) attribute responsibility for sadness to external circumstances. When we ourselves are responsible for a failure, the prevailing emotions are shame and a sense of guilt, while we feel angry when we blame a third person for the negative result.[7] Again with reference to cognitive antecedents, psychological literature points out that unhappiness does not derive from a simple setback, but from an *irrevocable* failure (Lazarus, 1991), where the subject is unable to reverse the negative situation. Failure can have two different kinds of connotations: it can arise in the absence of something desirable (i.e., a loss) or in the presence of something undesirable (i.e., some form of adversity). In many situations, a negative event

Table 2.1   Happiness and unhappiness: cognitive antecedents and action tendencies

	Cognitive antecedents	Action tendencies
Happiness	Desirability and certainty	Laughing, exuberance
Unhappiness	of the result	Renunciation, feeling lost, crying

can be interpreted both as a failure and as a form of adversity. For example, a student who fails an exam because she has a fever can curse her low score (loss) or her bad luck in having fallen ill at the wrong time (adversity). In this sense, psychologists note that sadness mainly derives from loss, while adversity tends to provoke anger.

In a world pervaded by hedonism and the pursuit of pleasure such as ours, it may seem bizarre to wonder about the function of sadness. In fact, people attempt to hide from the suffering that accompanies this negative emotion (Parrot, 2002). The answers provided by the cognitive scholars also reveal a certain discomfort: 'We have come to the first major case in which there is difficulty in postulating an action tendency' (Lazarus, 1991, p.251). According to Lazarus, the response to sadness is inaction, that is, 'not wanting', 'renunciation', 'feeling lost' and 'crying', as indicated in Table 2.1. When sadness is adaptive, the responses of inaction and renunciation perform a fundamental function for individuals attempting to recover a state of well-being. For the subject experiencing this emotion, unhappiness indicates the existence of a problem, of an irreversible negative situation. The inaction and 'withdrawal' of the unhappy person facilitate intense cognitive activity. The subject acknowledges the failure and accepts defeat, that is, she accepts the idea of abandoning the objective for which she has fought or in which she has invested. It is precisely this withdrawal that allows people to establish new and more attainable existential objectives: The sad person sees the world with different eyes (Izard, 1991). Lastly, sadness, like happiness, is an emotion that can strengthen social ties. Our unhappiness communicates to those around us that we are suffering due to something irreparable. As a result, this emotion normally elicits (at least in empathetic persons) the complementary emotion of compassion and hopefully the desire to help.

2.2   HAPPINESS, UNHAPPINESS AND CONSUMER BEHAVIOUR

Happiness pervades consumption nowadays. The material dimension of Western society views consumption as an existential objective, a craving that, once satisfied, is able to provide happiness. The 'consumption culture' describes a society that avidly wishes to consume for reasons that economists have traditionally defined as non-utilitarian; this attachment to material goods seems to completely ignore all higher social objectives and is therefore an end in itself. In particular, Richins and Dawson (1992) identify three dimensions of materialism: the central nature of purchasing, success as possession and the pursuit of happiness. Materialism is a real and proper lifestyle in which material goods and their purchase become the fulcrum of a person's existence. Moreover, the qualitative and quantitative dimensions of property reveal the lifestyle of a person to a materialistic society, thus signalling the success achieved by this individual. Lastly, the materialist does not seek happiness in relationships, but in consumption. Materialism is also described as an approach that considers possession to be the main source of happiness.

But does money buy happiness? In other words, is happiness based on consumption related to *life satisfaction*? The response given by sociological and marketing studies is ambiguous. The studies cited by Oatley (1992) show that poverty certainly makes people unhappy, while wealth supports well-being (but only within certain limits). In fact, it seems that Americans are no happier even if they earn twice as much as they did in the 1970s; not even the Japanese, who earn six times as much as they did in the 1950s, believe that their well-being has increased. Moreover, Richins and Dawson (1992) highlight an inverse relationship between material happiness and *life satisfaction*.

However, in line with the action tendencies connected with happiness, we would expect the joy connected with consumption to strengthen social ties. Both marketing and psychological studies have investigated this phenomenon and come to different conclusions. According to some scholars, for example, materialism is a useful *coping* tool for adolescents who have to face the anguish and distress arising from the separation of their parents. In fact, a number of distressing situations for children are associated with the separation of their parents, such as witnessing conflicts between the couple, possibly moving house and forced removal from friends and relatives, and a sense of abandonment. Consumption can therefore become an effective tool for dealing with the stress caused by a marriage crisis (Burroughs and Rindfleisch, 1997). Roberts et al. (2005) voice a different opinion, arguing that materialism and the happiness connected with this dimension increase family stress, and that the quest for happiness through possession does not prove to be an effective *coping* strategy for adolescents who spend their time on consumption rather than investing in family relationships.

Moreover, hedonistic happiness only prevails under certain conditions. In fact, it seems that certain contextual variables determine the level of joy in using goods or services: previous consumption experiences (Raghunathan and Irwin, 2001), the extent of the offer, and social influences (Raghunathan and Corfman, 2006).

Concerning the first of these variables, it has been demonstrated that the pleasure of previous consumption experiences affects the joy arising from the current use of a given product. For example, a tourist will find her fourth cruise particularly pleasant if the three previous cruises were not exhilarating; conversely, her happiness may be limited by unforgettable cruise experiences in the past, especially if each of those journeys exceeded her initial expectations and a positive consumption trend was therefore in place. These results have important and dramatic implications for marketing management, as 'consumers are always on a hedonic treadmill' (Raghunathan and Irwin, 2001, p. 356). It is precisely due to this 'inurement' to emotions, as already highlighted in Chapter 1, that studies on consumption happiness recognize the importance of adopting dynamic long-term strategies in order to charm consumers. In other words, companies have to regard consumer expectations as the outcome of an endless evolutionary process rather than a precise and static 'given' (Rust et al., 1999).

The variety of products and services on offer only ensures consumption happiness within certain limits. In fact, the selection of one option from an excessively vast range of offers can be demotivating and tiring, and can even prompt a customer to experience the emotion of regret in advance, a state arising from the customer's awareness of being unable to make the best choice.

BOX 2.1　THE CONSUMER'S AFFECTIVE AND COGNITIVE REACTIONS TO THE SOCIAL CONTEXT

Put yourself in the shoes of Maria Teresa, a cinema fan, who goes to see the latest film of a famous director with Alex, who is also a film enthusiast. At the end of the first half, Maria Teresa is really bored and disappointed, so she takes advantage of the intermission to communicate her negative judgement to Alex. However, before she can say a word, Alex exclaims enthusiastically: 'A masterpiece, don't you think?' Maria Teresa considers Alex a film expert, and her friend's opinion is likely to condition her judgement of the film positively (cognitive response). At the same time, this divergence of opinions and the relatively unpleasant state of dissonance will make this 'collective' consumption of art less pleasant for Maria Teresa (affective response).

Now imagine a different judgement by Alex. Before Maria Teresa can express her disappointment, Alex notes: 'How could such a great director stoop to such a low level?' In this case, his opinion will also influence his friend's cognitive and affective responses in different ways: Maria Teresa's negative judgement of the film will be reinforced, while their shared opinion will positively affect the pleasantness associated with the shared consumption experience.

It is also important to remember that many consumption activities, such as a holiday or a dinner at a restaurant, are very often collective experiences, meaning that the social context can also affect the pleasantness of these activities. A great deal of marketing literature has analysed how relations affect the consumers' *judgement* of an asset, but only more recent empirical research conducted by Raghunathan and Corfman (2006) has investigated the influence of the social context on the *joy* experienced by customers at the moment of consumption. This fine distinction between the consumer's affective and cognitive responses is illustrated in Box 2.1: in the case of collective consumption, the consistency of a person's judgement of an asset with that of other customers enhances the pleasure associated

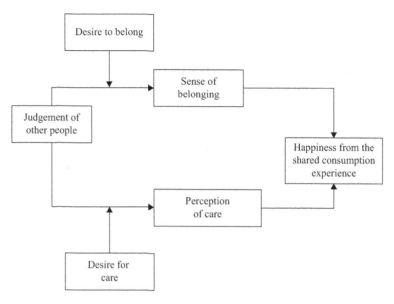

Source: Adapted from Raghunathan and Corfman (2006).

Figure 2.1   The influence of relations on consumption happiness

with consumption. On the other hand, disagreement will reduce the happiness connected with use, regardless of whether the opinion on the quality of the product is positive or negative.

In particular, as shown in Figure 2.1, two variables mediate the effect of other people's opinions on our happiness as consumers: the desire to belong and the desire for care. The desire to belong refers to the innate need to relate with other people, and the congruence of opinions naturally strengthens the sense of belonging. In contrast, the desire for care concerns the individual's need to ensure a correct representation of him or herself and of the surrounding environment. In this sense, the degree of agreement with other people's opinions affects the individual's perception of having made a correct judgement. These results sharply contrast with those obtained from emotive contamination theory (Howard and Gengler, 2001), which asserts that expressions of happiness by those who are near to us makes us joyful, thus positively conditioning our behaviour towards a product when this interaction takes place in a consumption context. For example, a smiling and enthusiastic assistant in a clothes shop will be able to positively condition the customers' behaviour towards the garments.

Like joy, unhappiness is also a shared consumption experience. This statement is particularly true of females. Compared to men, women have more negative purchase and consumption experiences and feel sadness and other connected emotions, such as anxiety, intolerance and stress, with greater frequency (Derbaix and Pham, 1991). As discussed in Chapter 4, the influence sadness exerts on customers is often compared with the effect of other negative emotions, such as anger. In particular, Raghunathan et al. (2006) conducted a study that compared the decision-making processes of anxious individuals to those of unhappy subjects. Anxiety is a negative emotion that is close to sadness in the sense that it shares its cognitive antecedents, with the exception of future expectations. The antecedent of sadness is *irreversible* loss, while that of anxiety is *probable* failure. When developed in a working or family environment, these emotive states have an impact on purchase and consumption choices. In particular, sad people are more inclined towards risk. In consumption, they mainly seek a 'compensation for loss' and not 'security and stability' as anxious people do.

Lastly, not only do happiness and sadness pervade the lives of consumers when they prepare to make a choice or to consume, but these emotions also form the basis of two advertising *appeals* that are frequently used to generate positive behaviour towards both the message and the advertised product.

Advertisers sometimes choose to combine these two communicational keys. One example is the well-known Dufour sweets campaign. The advertisement shows a girl in tears who unwraps a piece of candy in order to console herself, and it ends with the memorable *payoff*: 'It's not enough, but it helps'. In this case, the creatives intended to elicit what scholars define as mixed emotions (e.g., Hesapçı-Sanaktekin, 2007; Ursavas and Hesapçı-Sanaktekin, 2011). Is this a winning strategy? Not necessarily, according to Williams and Aaker (2002), who maintain that communications of this type can arouse discomfort in people who are less inclined to accept dualism, typically young people belonging to Western cultures. Appraisals, actions triggered by appraisals, marketing tactics and action tendencies for happiness are shown on Table 2.2.

Table 2.2   Happiness: appraisals, actions triggered by appraisals, marketing tactics, action tendencies

Happiness			
Appraisals	Actions triggered by appraisals	Tactic	Action tendencies
Desirability and certainty of the result	Acting on desirability in order to anticipate the state of happiness the consumer may feel when he or she experiences the product/service	Advertising may promise a state of happiness that arises from experiencing the service. This is the case of the typical advertisement for Disneyland where children's smiling faces show that they are living an exciting experience	Positive attitude toward the experience

2.3   A LUKEWARM VERSION OF HAPPINESS: SATISFACTION

As mentioned in Chapter 1, some scholars have classified different emotions using two-factor models. For example, emotions can be classified according to the dimensions of *pleasure* (displeasure) and *arousal* (lethargy). Therefore, the affective states concerning the dimensions of happiness and unhappiness can be classified according to their component of pleasantness and arousal. After establishing that happiness is characterized by the dimension of pleasure and unhappiness by that of displeasure, it is the arousal element that properly defines the emotions close to joy or sadness. For example, desperation and enthusiasm stand out due to the strong presence of the arousal component, while satisfaction and dissatisfaction have a more limited presence. As the common consumption experience is not usually an electrifying or dramatic event, we should not be surprised by the interest of scholars and marketing managers in *customer satisfaction*, one of the less intense forms of happiness.

But is satisfaction truly an emotion? If we refer to the features exhibited by the 'typical' emotion as presented in Chapter 1, the answer is certainly yes. With reference to marketing studies, Day

(1983), Woodruff et al. (1983), Sirgy (1984) and Cadotte et al. (1987) have interpreted satisfaction as a phenomenon with a predominantly emotive characteristic. In the psychological sphere, Shaver et al. (1987) demonstrate that satisfaction is an emotive subcategory of the wider dimension of joy, while Mehrabian and Russell's (1974) model described in Chapter 1 presents satisfaction as a component of pleasure. Satisfaction is also placed alongside happiness in numerous bipolar models (e.g., Watson and Tellegen, 1995). Therefore, in both marketing and psychological literature, 'there is much evidence to show that satisfaction is an emotion' (Nyer, 1997, p. 81).

Consumer satisfaction is considered an intangible strategic resource for a company, as it guarantees a long-term, sustainable competitive advantage. In particular, the competitive pressure and evolutionary dynamics of demand have emphasized the importance of this *asset*. This emotion is also of great interest because (albeit not precisely in agreement with the tendencies to action examined in the psychological sphere) satisfaction and dissatisfaction have been considered predictors of important post-purchase behaviour, such as repurchase and abandonment, positive and negative word of mouth, complaints and the like (Yi, 1989; Anderson and Fornell, 1994). Unfortunately for marketing managers, dissatisfaction does not determine a *particular* post-purchase behaviour. For example, according to Day (1983), in rare cases dissatisfaction implies complaint activity, a post-purchase behaviour that would instead be explained by other variables. Moreover, Day's conclusions are in line with the empirical results obtained in the psychological sphere and examined in section 2.1: the tendency to action triggered by unhappiness is 'inaction', and because dissatisfaction is an emotive state close to sadness it is difficult for the complaint to be an appropriate *coping* method for a dissatisfied customer. Similarly, customer satisfaction is not necessarily predictive of repurchase.

In order to understand precisely how customer satisfaction can be determined effectively by marketing activities, it is useful to analyse its cognitive antecedents, as is the case with the other emotions presented in the chapters that follow. The *appraisal* that determines this emotion is, of course, desirability, as satisfaction is a 'declension' of happiness. Concerning customer satisfaction in particular, product performance generates satisfaction when it exceeds standards; otherwise it elicits dissatisfaction (Howard and Sheth, 1969; Engel and Blackwell, 1982). Consumer behaviour scholars therefore consider this emotion to be the function of an initial standard, and the perception of a discrepancy may serve as the engine of satisfaction or the origin of dissatisfaction (Oliver, 1980). In fact, all of the various theories concerning customer satisfaction refer to this paradigm, which is known as confirmation/disconfirmation, but the theories differ in their identification of reference parameters.

One of these standards is customer *expectations*, which refer to overall performance and individual attributions of the offer. When compared to perceived performance, this set of expectations generates satisfaction or dissatisfaction (Tse and Wilton, 1998). Other models take consumer *desires* as a standard instead (Westbrook and Reilly, 1983): with reference to numerous purchase and consumption situations a divergence between customer expectations and desires is presumed to exist, and it is realistic to suppose that the latter can be responsible for ultimate satisfaction or dissatisfaction. A further standard involves *norms* (Cadotte et al., 1987), thus referring to an idea of average performance. Such norms are based on personal experience with a certain category of goods and on acquired information. Lastly, *perceived equity* can also be a parameter of the confirmation/disconfirmation theory (Oliver and Swan, 1989). Concerning this standard, the customer compares the costs/benefits of a purchase with those of the producer or service provider. Customer costs are typically the price of the product, the time taken to select the product, and so on, while the benefits are linked to performance. On the other hand, the supplier incurs costs, for example in the procurement of raw materials, and obtains an advantage in the sense that he or she makes a profit. Specifically, the perceived equity theory states that satisfaction and dissatisfaction derive from this comparison made by the consumer. The outputs presented in Box 2.2 show how the various standards described above contribute to generating customer satisfaction. The box shows excerpts from discussions with two focus groups aiming to investigate the origins of satisfaction among theatre-goers. When interviewed after seeing two famous plays, *King Lear* and *Who's Afraid of Virginia Woolf?*, the groups refer to more than one of the standards presented, thus demonstrating how varied the causes of this emotion can be.

Concerning the consequences of this particular emotion (and thus also the action tendencies it triggers), satisfaction is associated with repurchase (e.g., Oliver, 1980 and Oliver and Swan, 1989) and positive word of mouth (e.g., Gelb and Johnson, 1995), while dissatisfaction

BOX 2.2   CUSTOMER SATISFACTION: VARIOUS STANDARDS IN THE CONFIRMATION/ DISCONFIRMATION PARADIGM

King Lear

M: 'I was expecting a classical representation of *King Lear*. Instead, I was really pleased to see an original reinterpretation: it was all new and unexpected' [*satisfaction standard: expectations*].

S: 'I knew it wasn't a classical representation of Shakespeare, and this disturbed me a little. I thought I would feel out of place, not cultured enough to appreciate the interpretation. When I saw the room full of young people, I immediately felt at ease and knew I would enjoy myself' [*satisfaction standard: expectations*].

L: 'I didn't expect to be moved so much by the music. I was struck by the skill of the actors and the enthusiasm of the public' [*satisfaction standard: expectations*].

Who's Afraid of Virginia Wolf?

R: 'A car on stage! I've never seen anything like it at the theatre. Wonderful!' [*satisfaction standard: norms*].

F: 'Two euros for a small bottle of water! What thieves!' [*satisfaction standard: perceived equity*].

L: 'The cloakroom was expensive, too. It should have been included in the price of the ticket. . .what a disappointment' [*satisfaction standard: perceived equity*].

G: 'I wanted an entertaining evening. . .and instead I was bored to death' [*satisfaction standard: desires*].

Source: Adapted from Soscia and Turrini (2006).

can lead to abandonment of a supplier (e.g., Singh, 1990) or, in other cases, generate complaints (e.g., Hirschman, 1970) or negative word of mouth. Precisely because these various kinds of post-purchase behaviour have vastly different managerial implications, market-

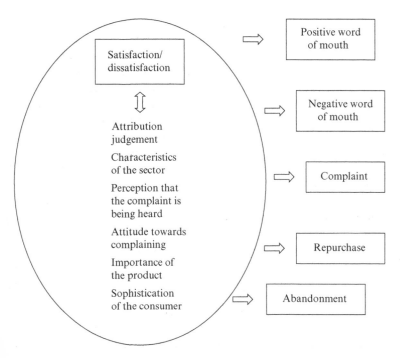

Figure 2.2   Relationship between consumer satisfaction and post-
purchase behaviour

ing literature has investigated the *conditions* that cause a satisfied or
dissatisfied customer to exhibit these particular types of behaviour.

As shown in Figure 2.2, the variables affecting the relationship
between satisfaction (and dissatisfaction) and post-purchase behaviour are *attribution judgement* (Krishnan and Valle, 1979), *characteristics of the sector* (Andreasen, 1985; Hirschman, 1970; Singh,
1990; Stephens and Gwinner, 1998), *consumer perception* that a
complaint has effectively been heard (Hirschman, 1970; Andreasen,
1985; Singh, 1990; Blodgett et al., 1995; Gelb and Johnson, 1995;
Singh and Wilkes, 1996; Stephens and Gwinner, 1998), *the customer's attitude towards complaining* (Blodgett et al., 1995; Keng et
al., 1995; Stephens and Gwinner, 1998), *the importance attached to
the product* (Blodgett et al., 1995), and *sophistication of the consumer*
(Hirschman, 1970; Gronhaug and Zaltman, 1977; Singh, 1990; Gelb
and Johnson, 1995).

Attribution judgement can be compared to the psychological concept of causation examined in Chapter 1: customers who negatively judge the performance of a product also question themselves regarding responsibility for this failure. They may hold themselves responsible for their dissatisfaction, or they may blame the manufacturer or adverse circumstances. As indicated in Chapter 1 and demonstrated at the end of this study, in the first two cases the consumer not only feels dissatisfaction, but also other negative emotions that help determine the post-purchase behaviour implemented.

Concerning the *characteristics of the sector*, the consumer only abandons the provider or producer that disappointed him or her if alternatives exist, that is, if a competitive situation exists. If, instead, a monopoly or oligopoly is in place, the exit barriers can be insurmountable, and the dissatisfied customer will only remain faithful because he or she is a 'prisoner'. For example, if we consider the passenger transport sector in Italy, we can suppose that a few Trenitalia customers are dissatisfied with the service. However, we can also assume that the *exit* option (in this case, travel by car or plane) is not easily accessible to many discontented customers.

Consumer perception that a complaint has been effectively heard determines the probability that a dissatisfied customer will contact the supplier for compensation. This is a very interesting consideration for marketing managers. In fact, it has been demonstrated that in addition to promoting contact with the supplier, this perception makes the consumer less likely to abandon the supplier for a competitor. Moreover, a provider who is willing to listen to complaints is able to prevent negative word of mouth effectively. In this sense, the initiative of various sales outlets that promise to reimburse their customers if they find the same garment elsewhere at a lower price is especially interesting. This promise is an important declaration of availability that should inhibit anticipated regret (and therefore promote the purchase), facilitate dialogue with the provider and make abandonment and negative word of mouth less likely.

On the other hand, *attitude towards complaining* refers to the individual inclination of the customer. As examined in the analysis of embarrassment and shame in Chapter 3, individuals are more or less inclined to complain in the case of dissatisfaction. Typically, certain socio-demographic variables can be used to identify customers who are less inclined to complain. Marketing studies have demonstrated that consumers who are willing to stand up for their rights are not young and have a high level of education and income. They are also assertive and self-confident. Those people who do not normally complain are more empathetic than those who protest. The former are inclined to put themselves 'in the shoes' of the people responsible for the disservice and therefore to justify such shortcomings. Psychological studies show that women are more empathetic than men, which could explain why they are more charitable when faced with a disservice.

The *importance of the product* concerns the value the customer attributes to an asset or service. This importance can be based on the price or simply on the affective value of the product. Marketing studies have demonstrated that the probability of a complaint increases with the importance of the asset.

Lastly, *consumer sophistication* expresses the customer's level of experience with reference to a particular sector, awareness of her rights as a consumer as well as knowledge of the methods for exercising them, and attention to the quality of the offer. People with a higher level of education and income are typically rather sophisticated consumers, and it has been demonstrated that a higher level of sophistication makes a complaint more probable in the case of dissatisfaction.

2.4 DESIRABLE HAPPINESS AND UNDESIRABLE SADNESS: HOPE AND FEAR

While satisfaction can be considered an indicator of happiness, there is an emotion close to (but markedly different from) joy that is of fundamental importance to the marketing sector: *hope*. Products such as pharmaceuticals and cosmetics base their very existence on the intangible resource of customer hope. The shrewdest marketing managers are well aware of its power. One example is the famous statement by the founder of Revlon: 'In the factory we make cosmetics; in the drugstore we sell hope'. Various consumption contexts, such as the lottery or the stock exchange, are strongly affected by this emotion.

From a cognitive standpoint, hope is a positive emotion with cognitive antecedents (such as joy) in the relevance and desirability of the output, but unlike happiness, hope also involves uncertainty.

Table 2.3   Hope and fear: cognitive antecedents and action tendencies

	Cognitive antecedents	Action tendencies
Hope	Desirability and uncertainty of the	Waiting
Fear	result	

The hoped-for event is *possible*, while the event that produces happiness is certain (Lazarus, 1991). Precisely with reference to the analysis of hope, MacInnis and De Mello (2005) highlight the difference between possibility and probability. The hopeful individual judges an event as possible even though it is improbable; therefore, the individual is a subject in waiting (see Table 2.3). This specification also allows us to distinguish hope from a closely related concept discussed above: expectation, which is instead based on probability.[8]

Considering the relevance of these tendencies to action, it comes as no surprise that advertisers attempt to manipulate the cognitive antecedents of hope to induce purchase and consumption behaviour. In advertising, the object of hope is typically a promise, either to interrupt an unfavourable situation or to achieve a favourable state.

The action triggered by the cognitive antecedents of hope makes it possible to reinforce these two situations and therefore to strengthen the customer's hope. In this regard, MacInnis and De Mello (2005) note how the communication strategies used to induce hope focus clearly on the desirability of the result or on the dimension of certainty.

With reference to the first *appraisal*, some marketing communications highlight the desirability of the result, promising improbable solutions to classical *trade-offs*, as is the case with certain slimming products that promise weight loss without any sacrifices. On the other hand, the importance of the result is emphasized by those campaigns that, for example, associate the promised benefits with a series of terminal values that make the expected result even more interesting and desirable. If the slimming product mentioned above is combined with the image of a happy couple, the benefit offered by the product is associated with the promise of a satisfying emotional life, that is, with a value that makes the product more *appealing*. Lastly, hope can be strengthened by targeting the *appraisal* of certainty, or in the words of MacInnis and DeMello (2005) by making the impossible become possible. In such cases, advertisers attempt to convince potential customers that certain goals, which are apparently difficult to achieve, are within reach. This communication strategy can be implemented by playing on the characteristics of the product, highlighting the consumer's possibilities or acting on the process, that is, indicating new or alternative methods of achieving a certain objective. Table 2.4 shows examples of tactics used in the various marketing proposals, which fuel hope as well as fear in potential customers.

Like hope, fear also implies the desire for a specific state (in this case, the desire to avoid a certain situation) and a cognitive belief attaching some probability to the situation (Ben-Ze'ev, 2000). Unlike hope, the evaluative component of this desire is negative. Nevertheless, *the presence of some probability* that the negative event will not occur forms the link between fear and hope (ibid.).

In general, fear has a negative connotation in consumer behaviour. In most situations, consumers are risk avoiders. Nevertheless, there are interesting exceptions, at least in the field of tourism. Research on sensation-seeking behaviour shows that certain consumers actively seek out fearful situations (Dolnicar, 2005).

Fear is the most commonly used negative emotion in advertising (Cochrane and Quester, 2005). According to the cognitive theory of emotions, fear appeal is a stimulus based on a threat. Public service advertising for AIDS, for example, focuses on the fear of death and engenders the emotional response of fright and discomfort (Soscia et al., 2012). In general, the fear appeal is organized in two parts (LaTour and Zahra, 1988): the creation of the fearful situation and the suggestion of a solution as a means of reducing fear.

There are numerous ways to classify fear appeals. In line with the categorization proposed by Cochrane and Quester (2005), these appeals rely on two approaches: fear of a negative consequence of *not using* the product (e.g., by not using condom one will get AIDS) and fear of a negative outcome associated with *using* a product (e.g., taking drugs). Both types of threat are physical in nature, but the fear may also refer to damage to the social image of the self (Spence and Moinpour, 1972), such as being considered a 'nerd' for not buying a specific brand. Finally, the different types of threats can also be industry-specific. For example, in tourism they identify the following categories (Dolnicar, 2005): political risk (e.g., terrorism),

Table 2.4 *Hope and fear: appraisals, actions triggered by appraisals, marketing tactics, action tendencies*

Hope

Appraisals	Actions triggered by appraisals	Tactic	Action tendencies
Desirability and uncertainty of the result	Acting on the appraisal of certainty: transforming the impossible into the possible	Nike: Just do it. The campaign pay off works specifically to transform the consumer into an athlete (who will only become one if he or she wants to)	Intention to buy is reinforced
	Acting on the appraisal of desirability: making an effect desirable	The effects of Tesmed, a brand of electro-stimulators – a strength training tool for sports people – are highlighted in the advertisements through the presentation of enviable, sculpted physiques	

Fear

Appraisals	Actions triggered by appraisals	Tactic	Action tendencies
Desirability and uncertainty of the outcome	Acting on the appraisal of certainty: showing a threat as a concrete potential negative outcome	TBWA in Paris has created anti-AIDS campaign where none other than the indestructible superheroes Superman and Wonderwoman are represented dying, suffering from the virus. The message is clear: AIDS also represents a real threat to superheroes	Intention to adopt correct behaviours
	Acting on desirability: Highlighting the non-desirability of the outcome	The previous example also shows the non-desirability of the wrong behaviour, portraying the outcome as the agony of death	

Source: Adapted in part from MacInnis and DeMello (2005).

environmental risk (e.g., natural disasters), health risk (e.g., lack of access to clean water), planning risk (e.g., unreliable tour operators) and property risk (e.g., theft). Of course, marketing managers may use advertising in order to reassure customers with regard to some of these threats.

With regard to this form of appeal and persuasion, the question is still widely debated in different marketing fields. In some fields, such as health policy, this question is a crucial one. For example, with regard to HIV/AIDS prevention campaigns, Green and Witte (2006) express the 'wish to bring fear appeals back into the AIDS discussion, and into research agendas to determine if, when, under what conditions, and how should fear appeals be used' (ibid., p. 257).

In spite of the many studies favouring fear appeals in AIDS communication, there are just as many that heavily criticize such appeals. Halperin (2006) maintains that the utilization of fear appeals alone may not be successful. O'Grady (2006) comments that using fear as the primary tool to reach populations is an incomplete approach to HIV/AIDS prevention, adding that 'resorting to scare tactics fails to motivate sustained behavioural change' (ibid., pp. 261–2). Kirby (2006) also criticizes Green and Witte's article and discusses the results of his own review of 83 studies on sex and HIV education programmes implemented worldwide. Kirby concludes that two-thirds of those programmes effectively reduced sexual risk-taking – by delaying sex, reducing the number of partners, or increasing condom use – on the basis of HIV risk and severity perception arousal methods. Finally, in a large interview-based study on condom use in Taiwan, Hsu (2006) shows that the effects of infection-fear appeals on predicting willingness to use condoms are insignificant. She suggests that merely increasing individuals' level of fear or worry is not enough to affect behavioural outcomes in HIV/AIDS prevention. Even if we do recognize that research supporting the use of fear appeals for persuasion is inconclusive, this type of appeal seems to be effective in terms of liking (La Tour and Pitts, 1989), attention and comprehension (Soscia et al., 2012).

In order to resolve this issue in relation to AIDS and other fields, it is important to understand how this appeal works and which variables are able to moderate its effectiveness. According to the 'protection motivation theory' (Roger, 1983), when an individual

faces a threat, there are four cognitive appraisals that elicit fear
and thus the action tendency: the severity of the threat; the perceived probability that the threat will be realized; coping response
efficacy, namely the ability of coping behaviour to neutralize the
threat; and self-efficacy, namely the individual's perceived ability
to perform the actions required to neutralize the threat. Tanner et
al. (1991) propose and empirically test an extended version of the
protection motivation theory, a framework that also accounts for
the role of a danger's social context. In this regard, Tanner et al.
(ibid.) state that adopting coping responses may have social implications in many contexts: 'For example, using a condom may imply
that one partner or the other has a sexually transmitted disease;
therefore, one may be reluctant to use the condom. The result
may be the adoption of maladaptive responses, and/or the feeling
of emotional distress when engaging in the dangerous behaviour'
(ibid., p. 40). Moreover, there are other variables that moderate
the effect of fear appeal, such as product involvement (Cochrane
and Quester, 2005), personality traits such as being a repressor (a
person who copes by avoidance or denial) or a sensitizer, namely
one who copes by engaging in extensive thought (Boyd, 1995), or
self-identity, such as hoped-for and feared selves (Patrick et al.,
2002).

Especially in social marketing, this predominant use of fear appeals
is criticized by marketing scholars who report the weaker effects or
the unintended deleterious effect of this appeal. Ethical concerns
about this communication tool include maladaptive responses such
as chronic heightened anxiety among those most at risk (Hastings et
al., 2004).

Hastings et al. (ibid.) suggest the use of positive appeals such
as humour and irony as an alternative to fear appeals in order
to elicit desired behaviours. In this regard, Soscia et al. (2012)
test the effectiveness of humour and fear in HIV/AIDS prevention advertising directed at young adults and generate different
recommendations. Their findings suggest that fear appeals are
far more effective than other appeals in HIV/AIDS prevention
advertising, while humour, an emotional stimulus widely used
for HIV/AIDS campaigns involving printed advertisements, has a
weaker effect.

Soscia et al. (ibid.) maintain that the superiority of the fear appeal
is especially pronounced in contexts where it has never been used

in AIDS prevention advertising. This is certainly the case in Italy, where informative and humour appeals have seen widespread use. In this regard, our suspicion is based on Helson's (1959) adaptation-level theory, which suggests that it is not only the focal stimulus (i.e., the advertising message) that determines perception, but also contextual stimuli (background) and residual stimuli (past experience). The individual learns to associate a set of stimuli with a reference point or adaptation level, and attention is generated when an object deviates from that point. This means that while a humorous ad might usually attract attention if it is surrounded by different approaches (e.g., based on fear), the ability of this stimulus to attract attention would be reduced if many humorous ads were used for AIDS prevention. On the other hand, advertising strategies that challenge the audience's expectations (adaptation level) will attract attention and leave an imprint on their memory. Thus, additional research is needed to verify the effect of humour appeals in contexts that do not have a history of humour as a standard strategy in prevention advertising.

Hope and fear appeals undoubtedly raise more serious issues of ethics compared with the other emotions we have analysed. These are subtle emotions that must be handled with responsibility and caution (Spence and Moinpour, 1972; Duke et al., 1993; Hastings et al., 2004). In order to tackle this problem and to decide on a case-by-case basis whether or not to use these appeals, if may be useful to follow the guidelines suggested by Duke et al. (1993), who developed an evaluation framework that aims to evaluate the ethics of fear appeals in specific cases. Their framework considers multiple stakeholders (e.g., society, organization and individual) and multiple ethical perspectives (e.g., utilitarian vs Kantian) in order to identify the trade-offs that characterize the use of fear appeals and thus to guide its use. Similar conflicts may arise when the hope appeal is chosen, in which case a managerial framework can also be developed as a conflict resolution technique.

2.5 THE MEMORY OF IRRETRIEVABLE HAPPINESS: NOSTALGIA

For marketing scholars, *nostalgia* is a positive sentiment towards objects (people, places or things) that were more common, popular or fashionable when a person was younger (Holbrook and Schindler, 2003). This does not mean that the object of nostalgia has disappeared or that it cannot be found. The nostalgic person may no longer use it for a particular reason; for example, a person may feel nostalgic about a chocolate egg they were crazy about when they were young, not because they are unable to buy it now (the product is still on the shelves), but because they avoid it in order not to gain weight.

Without a doubt, the fundamental characteristic of this emotion is its co-existence with a strong contradiction. In fact, nostalgia generates a bittersweet sensation, as it brings happy moments and pleasant memories to mind, but is also accompanied by the awareness that those moments are tied to an irretrievable past. Nostalgic people experience sensations of warmth, joy and pleasantness that intertwine with unpleasant states such as sadness and a sense of loss.

As indicated in Chapter 1, nostalgia is not elicited by the simple memory of a positive event or by the mere representation of what really happened, but rather by the consumer's historical and fanciful imagination.

Nostalgia can refer to events and circumstances that have not been experienced directly (Holbrook and Schindler, 2003). Therefore, the idea that there are various types of nostalgia – in which the person experiencing the sentiment takes on different roles – is becoming more deeply rooted: nostalgia can be real, simulated and collective.

When we speak of real nostalgia, we refer to the most typical nostalgia, namely that of a consumer who has personally experienced an event, met someone or possessed an object that generates this sensation. A typical example is the nostalgia aroused by a song that was popular during the years a person spent at university, connected with particular events and experiences that are fresh in the subject's memory.

Simulated nostalgia concerns a sentiment towards something that has not been experienced personally. Relationships between people come into play in this case, as it is precisely through interaction with other people and thanks to their stories that the consumer imagines the event, object or person about which he or she will feel nostalgic. By proposing images and stimuli of various kinds, for example, the mass media have transformed the experience of a few into the interest of many. This is how Woodstock has become an event with which even people who are too young to remember can identify.

Another type of simulated nostalgia is the historical variety, which is associated with objects and events that go so far back in time that they cannot have been socialized through interaction with the people who experienced them. One example of this phenomenon is the attachment of some art collectors to collections and museum items.

Lastly, there is also collective nostalgia, which may be connected with a culture, a country or certain symbols (national flags, particular religious celebrations and so on). This nostalgia is felt by entire groups of people who share the same values, the same historical background or the same cultural bases.

As mentioned above, people, places, events or goods can be the object of nostalgia. However, other people are most typically the object of this emotion. Regardless of whether they are no longer with us, or whether the events of life have caused their paths to diverge from ours, this emotion is very strong towards other people. Nostalgia may also be experienced for a place, such as one's country of origin, former stomping grounds, or places connected with pleasant moments and periods in life. Concerning events, nostalgia is often connected with situations that interrupt everyday life and routine. During a holiday, for example, certain moments remain etched in one's memory despite the passing of time. The fact that in most cases these moments are repeated every year makes them a fixed event, a pleasant situation that returns cyclically. When such habits cease, the feeling of nostalgia can explode rather violently.

In this context, goods merit separate treatment: cars, jewellery, books and toys can give rise to a vivid and important sentiment of nostalgia. Goods often allow a person to remember happy moments or particularly serene periods of life. Cars – especially one's very first car – bring the first taste of freedom to mind, youth and going out with girls and friends; jewellery may take people back to the moment when it was received as a gift; toys bring a sweet and carefree childhood to mind. The above applies even more to intangible goods. Songs, perfumes and films allow us to recollect particular moments in life (a hit song during one's school years, the heart-throb actor during one's teenage years, and so on). Therefore, instead of being real and proper objects of nostalgia, goods are stimuli for the historical imagination.

These nostalgic drifts run counter to a tendency examined in the second section of this chapter: materialism, the tendency to seek the satisfaction of purely hedonistic and material needs connected with the consumption of goods that satisfy immediate requirements and have strong social connotations. Rindfleisch et al. (2000) point out how materialism and nostalgia represent two irreconcilable ways of being. In particular, scholars investigate the automotive sector and demonstrate how people most inclined towards nostalgia prefer cars with a strong revival character, while those who are closer to materialism will choose cars that are synonymous with status.

The two tendencies, however, have a common denominator, viz. attention to the time of consumption. As discussed above, nostalgia is elicited from products, people or events from the past. Nostalgic people do not trust the present, and they give it a negative connotation. In contrast, materialism strongly accentuates the present: as maintained by Richins and Dawson (1992) and Rindfleisch et al. (1997), materialists seek instant gratification. They do not appreciate things from the past because they consider them old and unable to fully satisfy current needs.

As Solomon (1983) notes, products are consumed both for their social meaning (as symbols) and for their private meaning (as signs). Those highly inclined towards materialism will be interested in purchasing and consuming goods with a strong public and symbolic character, objects that others can admire and interpret. On the other hand, those who are highly inclined towards nostalgia will purchase goods of a very private and intimate nature.

In light of the latter considerations, marketing scholars advise marketing managers not to promote a product as both hedonistic *and* nostalgic. In fact, it appears that retro-status positioning (such as that used for the Plymouth Prowler in the car sector) is not a successful strategy. Nostalgic consumers dismiss these products as 'soulless', while materialists consider goods of this type to be outdated and incapable of gratifying the socio-psychological need they wish to satisfy.

On the basis of several examples, Table 2.5 summarizes the role played by the emotions presented in the various purchase and consumption phases.

Table 2.5   Role played by satisfaction, hope, fear and nostalgia in the purchase and consumption processes

	Emotions		
	Happiness/unhappiness	Hope and fear	Nostalgia
Phases of the purchase and consumption process	*EXAMPLES*		
Perception of need, search for information and assessment of alternatives	The strategic objective of the Disneyland advertisement briefly described in Table 2.2 was to shift attention from the service characteristics to the result of well-being and satisfaction, anticipating the happiness that potential customers can experience at Disneyland	The advertising for Kilocal Program 221 arouses hope in overweight women that they can lose weight quickly and without major sacrifices	'Certain things are even better than I remember them' is the nostalgic headline of the Jiffy Pop popcorn ad
Moment of purchase	Satisfaction (or dissatisfaction) can be experienced at the moment of purchase, for example through the product test. Think of marketing activities such as the 'Doors open for Renault' campaign, where users were allowed to test drive the cars on display	Similarly, a dietician or pharmacist can generate hope when a diet supplement is purchased	The setting of the Ralph Lauren stores, which is reminiscent of certain old villas, connects the moment of purchase with nostalgia

Table 2.5 (continued)

	Emotions		
Phases of the purchase and consumption process	Happiness/unhappiness	Hope and fear	Nostalgia
		EXAMPLES	
Moment of consumption	The use of any product can generate satisfaction or dissatisfaction	The use of an anti-cellulite product is certainly an example of hopeful consumption Information printed on cans and bottles to remind consumers to drink responsibly may use the fear appeal	Listening to an oldies radio station can be nostalgic consumption
Phases subsequent to purchase and consumption	In Chapter 5, we will examine how satisfaction and dissatisfaction are necessary but insufficient conditions for certain types of post-purchase behaviour, such as word of mouth	Social campagns that recommend having a designated driver may use the fear appeal	Real nostalgia is an antecedent of faithfulness

NOTES

1. The distinction between the two emotions happiness and joy is very fine, and I do not consider it relevant to the analysis of consumer behaviour. For this reason, the distinction is disregarded in this study. Readers interested in the differences should read Lazarus (1991).
2. The emotion of pride will be examined in Chapter 3.
3. Gratitude will be analysed in Chapter 4.
4. In this case as well, I do not consider the managerial implications of this distinction to be relevant. Readers interested in analysing the link between joy and love should consult Oatley (1992), while the marketing implications of love are discussed by Batra et al. (2012).
5. Cited in McMahon (2006).
6. The concept of empathy will be analysed in Chapter 3.
7. Social emotions, including guilt and shame, will be analysed in Chapter 3, while anger will be dealt with in Chapter 4.
8. In this sense, it should be specified that while hope is an emotion, expectations are convictions. Moreover, expectations imply the assignment of a probability to an event that may be positive or negative, while hope only concerns desirable events (MacInnis and De Mello, 2005).

3. Pride and sense of guilt

This chapter examines the emotions of guilt and pride, both of which are known as social emotions. With regard to the appraisal of agency examined in the first chapter, we notice that these emotions are elicited by the self. The chapter also analyses feelings of guilt, an emotion we experience when we violate a rule and blame ourselves for the violation. Following a purely psychological study of this state and after distinguishing guilt from two similar states – shame and embarrassment – this chapter discusses how these powerful emotional tools are managed by marketers. The chapter ends by taking a look at pride, an emotion specular to guilt: in this case, the self is responsible for a favourable event. Pride is, therefore, a positive emotion, but – as illustrated below – it does not always affect marketing activities favourably.

3.1 SENSE OF GUILT: COGNITIVE ANTECEDENTS AND TENDENCIES TO ACTION

Guilt is an emotion that pervades our existence. According to Baumeister et al. (1994), we experience this emotion for at least two hours every day. It is certainly a painful yet reassuring presence: its absence would inevitably plunge any society into catastrophic anarchy. Guilt plays a fundamental adaptive role in human life, as it acts as a powerful tool of socialization in preserving and maintaining social ties (ibid.). This affective state is classified as *social emotion* or *moral emotion* (Tangney and Dearing, 2002) since it requires the capacity to reflect on one's actions and to assess it in relation to the social norms and the set of interpersonal relations to which the subject belongs.

The sense of guilt is commonly defined as 'regret or remorse for not having acted according to one's conscience' (Ferguson, 1999,

p. 308). However, it is important to point out that guilt itself does not necessarily imply a sense of guilt (Sabini and Silver, 1998). Where a sense of guilt is absent, a person who suffers a wrong can attempt to induce a sense of guilt in the wrongdoer. In this context, Miceli and Castelfranchi (1998) classify three types of *guilt trip*: *direct accusation*, *indirect accusation* and *forgiveness*; the third type, according to Miceli and Castelfranchi, is certainly the most cunning and effective way of generating a sense of guilt.

Direct accusation is an assertive and intentional system of inducing guilt: in this case, the 'victim' openly confronts the guilty person with her wrongdoings. Suppose, for example, that Stefano, Luciana's boyfriend, forgets her birthday. Let us try to feel the disappointment, anger and frustration she feels. Luciana could make Stefano feel guilty by attacking him directly with an accusation such as: 'Considering it's my birthday, I was expecting at least a bunch of flowers! But you do not care . . . '. Alternatively, Luciana could induce Stefano to reflect on his wrongdoings by putting on a contrite air and refusing to talk to him for the whole evening; or, she could *nonchalantly* turn the conversation to the unhappiness of women who are neglected by their companions. In these cases, the accusation is indirect, a recrimination articulated through non-verbal behaviour or through vague and faraway references to the failings of the accused person. Lastly, Luciana could 'forgive' Stefano for his misdeed. For example, she could assume her companion's point of view by coming out with a phrase such as, 'Come on! A birthday's not important!'. Or she could give him an easy justification for his failure: 'With all the trouble you're going through at the moment, it's obvious you didn't want to worry about my birthday as well!'. It goes without saying that forgiveness as a means of inducing a sense of guilt is only effective when the accused person is sufficiently empathetic. If Stefano were not so, for example, he would be led to believe he had *truly* been pardoned by Luciana, and that was certainly not her intention. The relationship between a sense of guilt and empathy has important social as well as marketing implications, and it will therefore be analysed in section 3.3.

One can also *feel* guilty without actually *being* guilty at all (Sabini and Silver, 1998). We must not forget that expressing particular emotions, even if not truly perceived, plays a fundamental role in our presentation of ourselves to other people. Guilt in particular can be expressed in order to highlight our moral stature (ibid.). Imagine, for example, that Stefano remembers Luciana's birthday and he gives her a splendid bunch of flowers. Stefano could, however, feel uncomfortable and express his discomfort to Luciana: 'Certainly, the occasion was so important that we should have celebrated your birthday with a party, I'm sorry I didn't think about it'. In such a scenario, Stefano, who has done his minimum duty as a boyfriend, is 'authorized' not to be sorry for not having organized a party and for not communicating his sense of guilt. A statement of this type, however, makes him even more special for Luciana, and he is certainly aware of this.

According to the macro-classification of the appraisals proposed in Chapter 1, feelings of guilt are elicited by an undesirable event caused by the self. Additional specific antecedents of guilt include the violation of a rule and the ability to prevent such a violation.

The sense of guilt is described as a 'dysphoric state associated with the recognition of the violation of an important moral or social rule' (Kugler and Jones, 1992, p. 318). In reality, a breach that elicits a sense of guilt does not necessarily involve a moral or a social rule (Ben-Ze'ev, 2000) such as the importance of celebrating a birthday. For example, let us try to imagine the emotions felt by Arianna, a girl who set out to lose weight and who yields to the temptation of a gratifying slice of chocolate cake. Arianna will probably feel guilty even though she has not offended anyone. It is also difficult to imagine that someone else forced the girl to interrupt her diet; instead, she has to sadly take responsibility for her transgression. In fact, an individual who feels guilty accepts responsibility for breaking the rules and does not attribute the transgression to others (Tangney and Dearing, 2002). Lastly, the sense of guilt experienced by Arianna derives from the fact that the girl recognizes that she could have prevented her transgression: when deciding how to satisfy her appetite, she preferred a slice of chocolate cake to a healthy but less interesting fruit salad. Therefore, this emotion is not simply elicited by one's responsibility for the breach of a rule, but also by a person's awareness of the possibility of self-regulation (Izard, 1977; Baumeister, 2002).

With specific reference to the latter antecedent to the sense of guilt, namely the ability to prevent transgressions, psychology literature highlights that this emotion can be experienced before the breach takes place. In this case, it is referred to as anticipated guilt. Imagine, for example, that Arianna feels guilty when she accepts the offer of

Table 3.1   Guilt: appraisals and action tendencies

Appraisals	Action tendencies
Violation	Confession of the violation
Self-responsibility	Search for justifications
Ability to prevent the violation	Attempt to remedy the situation
	Intention not to commit the same transgression in future
	Denial

a slice of cake even before she tastes it. Therefore, it is possible to experience this emotion in response to the mere thought of 'behaving badly'. Unlike the sense of guilt, the concept of *anticipated guilt* has not been the subject of in-depth psychological studies (Massi Lindsey, 2005). However, as indicated below, it is a very interesting affective state from a marketing point of view, as we will see in the following section. As mentioned above, the feeling of guilt is an unpleasant and distressing sensation. For this reason, those who feel this emotion are prompted to take action in order to mitigate their suffering. From a functionalist point of view, guilt plays precisely this role: it motivates and prepares 'guilty' people to act in such a way as to re-establish the social links threatened by their violations (Kugler and Jones, 1992; Tangney and Dearing, 2002). Guilt prepares the action that Frijda et al. (1989) define as 'help' (see Table 3.1).

In this sense, the most typical tendencies to action in response to a sense of guilt are confessing to the violation, attempting to remedy the situation, searching for justification or, in Arianna's case, firmly intending not to commit the same transgression in the future (Tangney and Dearing, 2002). Denial is regarded as a less common action tendency compared to the others. These tendencies are mentioned among the coping methods listed in Table 3.1: confessing the violation is a form of accepting responsibility – an attempt to remedy the situation – and the intentions are 'planned problem-solving' methods, while denial is a coping tool geared toward escape.

Feelings of guilt can certainly be distressing, and the anticipated sense of guilt can likewise cause suffering. For this reason, those who feel guilty in advance are induced to take action to limit this suffering, such as deciding not to violate the rule or formulating convincing arguments in order to justify the imminent violation.

3.2   SENSE OF GUILT AND CONSUMER BEHAVIOUR

The sense of guilt is an emotion that has been widely neglected by marketing studies (Burnett and Lunsford, 1994; Dahl et al., 2003). Nevertheless, marketing managers and marketing communication managers often use this emotion to promote goods and services. For example, Huhmann and Brotherton (1997) demonstrate that the sense of guilt is used in advertising just as frequently as communicational appeals that have been studied for decades, such as humour and fear.

With particular reference to consumer behaviour, Dahl et al. (2003) investigated this negative emotion by conducting descriptive research in which they asked respondents to recollect and recall a consumption experience involving a sense of guilt. In this way, the scholars identified three types of situations that were potentially affected by this state. Consumers can feel guilt towards another person, towards themselves or towards society as a whole.

Burnett and Lunsford (1994) also classified different types of consumer guilt-inducing circumstances by suggesting four categories: financial, health, moral and social responsibility. Financial guilt may arise when a consumer bears the costs of unneeded or extravagant goods or purchases that she is not able to justify easily. Health guilt emerges when a customer believes that she is not taking care of her physical well-being. Moral guilt comes about when a consumer feels that her purchase decisions violate a particular ethical guideline or moral imperative (e.g., drinking alcohol when it is forbidden by one's religion or other values). Social responsibility guilt is experienced when the purchase decision transgresses one's perceived obligations to others (e.g., not donating to a charity).

In the first case quoted by Dahl et al. (2003), consumers experience this negative emotion when they notice that their purchase decisions may have a negative impact on the people close to them. One example could be a husband who feels guilty towards his wife for making a major purchase without consulting her first, or a father who, after treating himself to a luxury item, feels he has deprived his children. According to Burnett and Lunsford (1994), these situations may elicit *financial guilt*.

Marketing managers are aware that this emotion can pose a major obstacle to the purchase of 'superfluous' items, and some luxury brands, such as Patek Philippe, have skilfully overcome this unpleasant emotion by suggesting cunning and convincing purchase justifications and thus modifying the appraisal set. The advertisement suggests that the transgression is not effective: as a matter of fact, the 'transgressor' is actually making an investment buying the precious watch in order to leave it to the next generation. Scholars have demonstrated that gift-with-purchase promotions can also reduce guilt by counterbalancing feelings of self-indulgence (Lee-Wingate and Corfman, 2010). Naturally, *not* taking a consumption decision can also cause serious problems for other people; this is shown by certain social campaigns aiming to promote the use of contraceptives, to name but one example.

In the second situation mentioned by Dahl et al. (2003), the consumer feels guilty because she has not acted consistently with the values and principles of the person she would like to be. This could be the case with Arianna, for example, who, yielding to the temptation of the chocolate cake, feels guilty because she is aware that she is compromising her figure and, perhaps, her health in the long term. According to Burnett and Lunsford (1994), this is a case of *health guilt*. Nevertheless, actions that are inconsistent with values may also elicit *moral guilt*. In this case, marketing managers are also able to promote indulgence by providing justifications and thus manipulating the antecedents of consumer guilt by declaring that a guilty pleasure is low in calories, to name one example.

In the third case presented by Dahl et al. (2003), the violation of a social standard is considered. According to Burnett and Lunsford (1994), this transgression elicits *social guilt*. In this type of transgression, the consumer will feel guilty, for example, if she does not recycle or decides not to support a humanitarian cause. This was the case in the 'Un Techo para Chile 2011' campaign. This non-profit organization was founded in 1997 to provide housing for the poor and relies on donations from corporations, families and students to cover its operating costs. Taking better care of animals than people is considered immoral by nearly everybody, and the Un Techo para Chile 2011 campaign appeals to this rule: its headline reads 'There are thousands of families that are not as lucky as your pet is'. Many social campaigns promote a particular cause by playing on the potential contributors' sense of guilt. This appeal, however, is sometimes also used by *profit*-oriented businesses. For example, when reminding potential car purchasers that buying a foreign car damages the Italian economy, Fiat intends to induce an anticipated feeling of guilt for doing harm to their own country.

How does the guilt-lacerated consumer behave? What action does she take to reduce her discomfort? In line with the functionalistic outlook introduced in section 3.1 (see Table 3.1), Dahl et al. (2003) identify *amendment and commitment* as the type of action most frequently used to this end. In this case, the consumer makes amends for her wrongdoings by taking reparatory action (e.g., returning an object she cannot afford to the shop) or compensatory action, such as donating money to charity after buying a luxury item or buying from a for-profit company that supports non-profit organizations. Alternatively, the repentant buyer can promise not to transgress in the future. The authors also identify a second tendency to act that they defined as *acknowledgement and rationalization*. In this second case, consumers are led to confess their transgressions to other people and to seek comfort and, in particular, justification of their behaviour from their interlocutors. The third action tendency identified by the authors, *denying and denigrating*, is the least frequent. In this case, the consumer attempts to remove the perhaps rash purchase and consumption choices, refuses to take responsibility for the event, or – in very rare cases – alcohol, bulimic behaviour or drug-taking may even help him or her overcome the discomfort accompanying the sense of guilt.

The consumer guilt situations identified in the marketing literature have led company managers, depending on the circumstances, to induce this negative emotion in potential purchasers or instead to mitigate this emotion. For example, volunteers for the Galens Medical Society, a non-profit organization managed by medical students at the University of Michigan, play on a sense of guilt in their potential subscribers in order to collect funds for helping children in need: the students decided to collect money opposite Zingerman's, the most refined delicatessen in Michigan, where those who cheerfully spend dollar upon dollar on delicious food should be ready to help the less fortunate. In many cases, it is advertising that conveys this persuasive intention. For example, Telefono Azzurro, a foundation that provides assistance to abused children, used advertising to communicate to its potential subscribers that without their immediate action they would soon be unable to deliver the service. The foundation therefore used what marketing literature defines as a *guilt-arousing appeal*, a communication strategy aiming at eliciting

guilt in the audience, an emotion that can probably induce reparatory or compensatory actions such as the donation of money.

In contrast, the above-mentioned example related to the Patek
Philippe brand illustrates the use of a *guilt-decreasing appeal*, a
mechanism designed to reduce the sense of guilt felt by potential
purchasers of luxury watches, a feeling that may well be an obstacle to this type of outlay. This may also be the case in the majority
of corporate social responsibility initiatives (Chang, 2008). It has
become a major trend in corporate philanthropy to donate money
to a charity each time a consumer makes a purchase (ibid.). Gucci
consumers, for example, may be aware that in 2011 Gucci donated
25 per cent of the retail price from all sales of the special edition
'Gucci for UNICEF' Sukey bag to support UNICEF's 'Schools for
Africa' programmes in Malawi and Mozambique, where nearly one
million children have been orphaned by HIV/AIDS. In this case,
the company helped consumers make effective guilt-reducing arguments. Table 3.2 summarizes the consumer appraisals, appraisals
acting, tactics used by marketing managers and consumer action
tendencies discussed above.

Are these appeals effective? Research in the field of advertising
has attempted to provide answers to this question (Bozinoff and
Ghingold, 1983; Coulter and Pinto, 1995; Bennett, 1998; Cotte et al.,
2005; Basil et al., 2006). Bozinoff and Ghingold (1983) were among
the first marketing scholars to investigate the sense of guilt as an
advertising appeal, and they verified the capacity of advertising to
elicit this emotion. However, the two authors demonstrate the inef-
ficiency of *guilt-arousing appeals* in conditioning brand behaviour or
purchase intentions and attribute this failure to the formulation of
possible counter-arguments by the recipients. In this sense, Cotte et
al. (2005) underline how the perception of a manipulative intent by
the source is a possible counter-argument that can weaken the effectiveness of a guilt-arousing appeal; this perception can even have
negative effects on brand image. Moreover, besides the manipulative
intent, scepticism about advertising tactics and the credibility of the
specific ad may also influence the level of guilt perceived and thus
also consumer behaviour (Hibbert et al., 2007).

Coulter and Pinto (1995) also demonstrate that only communicational appeals that elicit a moderate sense of guilt are effective.
In line with these findings, Jiménez and Yang (2008) demonstrate
that consumers show more favourable attitudes towards green

Table 3.2 Consumer guilt: appraisals, actions triggered by appraisals, marketing tactics, action tendencies

Guilt			
Appraisals	Actions triggered by appraisals	Tactic	Action tendencies
Violation Self-responsibility Capacity to prevent the violation	Acting the violation in order to deny the transgression (guilt-decreasing appeal)	Decreasing financial guilt: in the case of Patek Philippe, the transgressor is actually making an investment Decreasing health guilt: the consumer that drinks Voli, light vodkas promoted as having up to one-third fewer calories than leading brands, is actually taking care of himself/herself physically	Intention to commit the transgression is reinforced
	Acting the violation, responsibility and capacity to prevent to emphasize the transgression (guilt-increasing appeal)	Increasing social guilt: Fiat, for example, reminds potential car purchasers that buying a foreign car damages the Italian economy Increasing health guilt: e.g., anti-smoking campaigns that remind smokers that their behaviour harms others and themselves Increasing financial guilt: e.g., an insurance company that advises consumers not to waste money so that they can afford insurance for their children's education	Intention to commit the transgression is weakened

advertisements and advertised brands when they are exposed to a low-guilt advertisement than to a high-guilt one. In fact, inducing a strong sense of guilt is sometimes accompanied by irritation and anger, emotions that have a negative impact on brand behaviour and that discourage purchases.

The aforementioned studies on using the sense of guilt in advertising were limited to checking the effectiveness of guilt-arousing appeals and, with rare exceptions (e.g., Coulter and Pinto, 1995), the analysis was limited to the *non-profit* sector. However, as indicated in the Patek Philippe watch advertisement, for example, *guilt-decreasing appeals* are also widely used in the field of advertising and mainly involve the *profit* sector. This is a communication strategy that sets out to 'tempt' the potential purchaser by suggesting a convincing purchase justification. Marketers try to help customers make guilt-reducing arguments by offering justifications (Lee-Wingate and Corfman, 2010). It is no coincidence that the editorial prepared to promote the Ford 500 and the Chrysler 300 is entitled 'Guilt-free luxury' (*Entrepreneur*, October 2005). It is also no coincidence that the headline chosen to promote a new syrup for the preparation of sweets is 'Indulgence minus the guilt factor' (*Food Manufacture*, October 2005). With some exception such as the study conducted by Soscia et al. (2007), marketing literature has not investigated the effectiveness of guilt-decreasing appeals. Not only do those authors demonstrate the effectiveness of this communication tactic, but they also point out how this lever does not compromise the hedonistic dimension of a *guilty pleasure*.

Apart from advertising, the literature and marketers suggest several tactics that can reduce the guilt frequently associated with the consumption of luxuries or non-essential consumptions. With regard to promotions, scholars demonstrate that gift-with-purchase promotions may decrease guilt by counterbalancing self-indulgence or by creating a favourable comparison with another's consumption (Lee-Wingate and Corfman, 2010). Low-fat nutrition labels may also be an effective marketing tool capable of decreasing the guilt of a consumer who wishes to treat him or herself to snack foods (Wansink and Chandon, 2006). Moreover, in the recreation industry, the 'all-inclusive' strategy to promote resorts is a viable way to eliminate the guilt associated with costly, pleasurable activities during a vacation by allowing guests to prepay all expenses (Kivetz and Simonson, 2002; Rayna and Striukova, 2009).

3.3 THE RELATIONSHIP BETWEEN GUILT, SHAME AND EMBARRASSMENT: IMPLICATIONS FOR CONSUMER BEHAVIOUR

Shame and embarrassment are two other social emotions that can be confused with the sense of guilt. In particular, the distinction between guilt and shame was studied in depth by Tangney and Dearing (2002). Previous analyses theorized that the difference between guilt and shame mainly lies in the presence or absence of witnesses to a weakness or shortcoming: therefore, while guilt can be experienced privately, shame is only experienced in the presence of other people.

Tangney and Dearing (2002) empirically demonstrated that the two emotions do not differ depending on the presence of an audience, nor do they differ on the basis of the type of transgression committed. Rather, it seems that shame implies a reflection on oneself, while guilt is elicited by a judgement of the shortcoming or the action committed. Therefore, while the cognitive antecedent of guilt is the thought 'I did something wrong', shame is accompanied by the judgement 'I am wrong' (ibid.). Consequently, guilt does not involve an attack on the self through global devaluation, while shame does trigger such an attack.

For this reason, shame is a more painful experience than guilt and implies different tendencies to action. As discussed above, a sense of guilt induces the guilty party to excuse him or herself, to confess or to remedy, while those who feel shame wish to hide or escape. In particular, with reference to Table 3.3, Frijda et al. (1989) identify 'blushing' and 'hiding from sight' as behavioural consequences of shame and embarrassment. Therefore, it is no coincidence that suicide is an extreme consequence of shame rather than guilt (Lazarus, 1991).

Table 3.3   Shame and embarrassment: appraisals and action tendencies

Appraisals	Action tendencies
Violation of a social rule and presence of an audience	Blushing Hiding from sight Escape/avoidance

BOX 3.1 EMPATHY AND SOCIAL
CONSUMPTION EMOTIONS

In line with the definition of emotion provided in the first chapter, we do not consider empathy an emotion, but rather an ability, an individual capacity to experience emotions (Lazarus, 1991). More precisely, according to Eisenberg and Fabes (1990, p.132), empathy is 'an emotional response that stems from another emotional state or condition, is congruent with the other's emotional state or condition, and involves at least a minimal degree of differentiation between self and other'.

If we refer to negative emotions, empathy is the 'strong awareness of another person's suffering accompanied by the need and desire to mitigate such suffering' (Bagozzi and Moore, 1994, p.59). With reference to consumer behaviour studies, the relationship between guilt and empathy was the subject of an investigation into the effectiveness of *guilt-arousing appeals* in promoting the collection of funds by charities (Basil et al., 2006). Basil et al. demonstrated, for example, that the sense of guilt felt by a potential supporter of a humanitarian cause is not, by itself, sufficient to ensure that person's support. Instead, this sense of guilt only has effective communicational appeal when it is accompanied by a state of empathy. Bagozzi and Moore (1994) reached the same conclusion: the negative emotions aroused by a social campaign motivate people to support the cause only when empathy acts as a mediating variable.

Another possible tendency to action associated with shame is attributing one's responsibilities to third parties: blaming other people rather than oneself for a shameful action allows the person to restore her sense of self-value. For this reason, shame can sometimes turn into *anger* towards those who witness the shameful action or are victims of it, while a sense of guilt is frequently accompanied by a sense of *empathy* (see Box 3.1) towards those who are harmed by the shortcoming or transgression (Tangney and Dearing, 2002).

Therefore, according to Tangney and Dearing (2002), there is no doubt that the adaptive function of the sense of guilt is more important than that of the shame precisely because the sense of guilt – unlike shame – involves an empathetic dimension.

This conclusion was strongly criticized by Sabini and Silver (1998), who instead emphasized the educational role of such a distressing emotion as shame: specifically because guilt is accompanied by less suffering: '[I]t isn't powerful enough to counter serious temptation. . . . Bad character needs to be nipped in the bud before seriously bad things happen. . . . So, Tangney's program for the abolition of shame is not merely impossible but imprudent' (Sabini and Silver, 1998, p. 93). Moreover, the authors highlight how the distinction between guilt and shame is often finer and more ambiguous than that proposed by Tangney and Dearing (2002).

This debate on the function of shame is relevant to social marketing. In line with Sabini and Silver (1998), de Hooge et al. (2008) solve the apparent paradox concerning the function of shame by demonstrating that this painful emotion (as well as guilt) motivates prosocial behaviours when its experience is relevant to the decision at hand. On the other hand, studies in social advertising do not arrive at the same conclusion. It seems that shameful responses among the target audience produce negative consequences (Bennett, 1998). These contrasting findings suggest the need for further studies on the potential positive interpersonal function of shame in social marketing.

Less ambiguous and more positive conclusions come from health and public marketing studies that analyse the effect of shame in reducing harmful behaviours such as alcohol abuse (Agrawal and Duhacheck, 2010) and in reinforcing self-control (Chun et al., 2007). Agrawal and Duhacheck (2010) demonstrate that shame appeals as well as guilt appeals are effective in influencing behavioural intentions only if the same emotion is not incidentally experienced by the consumer prior to ad exposure. Consumers exposed to message frames that elicit the same emotion are motivated by emotion repair and tend to process the advertisements in a defensive manner. With regard to self-control, Chun et al. (2007) prove that consumers who anticipate shame from consuming a hedonic product will be more likely to engage in self-control than consumers who anticipate guilt. These results should not surprise the reader; as discussed above, guilt gives rise to the possibility of justifications and atonement for one's wrongdoings; shame does not. Interestingly, in 2009 the same scholars demonstrated that pride is even more powerful than shame in facilitating resistance to temptation, as we will discuss in the next section.

The different tendencies to action associated with guilt and shame (see Table 3.1 and Table 3.3) are extremely important and interesting reactions from a consumer behaviour perspective. For example, shame strongly affects the choice of complaint methods used by dissatisfied consumers (Mattila and Wirtz, 2004). As discussed in Chapter 5, complaining is a relevant consequence of dissatisfaction. According to Mattila and Wirtz (ibid.), people who complain can have two objectives: they may simply wish to air their dissatisfaction, or they may demand compensation for the disservice. The authors demonstrate that in the second case, the consumer will manifest her dissatisfaction using direct complaint methods: she will take it out on the *front desk* either in person or over the phone.

In the first case, the consumer will instead choose less direct, more distant and detached methods, such as a letter or an e-mail. At the same time, the study shows that shy consumers choose the indirect complaint method regardless of whether they demand compensation or simply wish to vent their anger. Shy people, in fact, do not complain directly but rather wish to conceal themselves. For this reason, from the company's point of view a shameful consumer is potentially more dangerous than an angry one. The latter will give the company the opportunity to remedy the problem, the former will not. As we will discuss in the next chapter, when angry customers are given an appropriate channel for expression, this emotion may benefit the company's relationship with the customer. Mattila and Wirtz (2004) advise marketing managers to encourage direct complaints in order to discourage shameful consumers from engaging in post-purchase behaviour that can damage the company, such as negative word of mouth and even boycotting. Nevertheless, when a consumer's loss of self-esteem is serious at the end of a brand relationship, it may be time to give up. Sometimes trying to win a customer back can even exacerbate the situation (Johnson et al., 2011). This has seemingly extreme managerial implications: a company would be better off making sure that shameful customers who abandon the brand find a new and happy home with another firm (ibid.). The scholars claim that the sooner the customers are happily involved with a new brand, the faster one might expect damage to their self-concept to be repaired and faster the motive to harm the offending firm might dissipate (ibid.).

In the for-profit sector, purchase and consumption processes are more frequently affected by a sense of embarrassment than shame. Compared to shame, embarrassment is a weaker emotive reaction, and it derives from violations of lesser importance (Ben-Ze'ev, 2000). It is therefore an emotion that can commonly affect a consumer's life. In fact, although it may be difficult for readers to recall a purchase or consumption experience in which they felt ashamed, they will certainly remember their embarrassment when their credit card was not accepted for a payment.

This episode allows us to highlight two important cognitive antecedents of embarrassment that distinguish it from shame and guilt: embarrassment involves violating a social rather than a moral norm and requires an *audience* (ibid.). The inability to make a payment is not a moral offence, and the embarrassment is generated by the fact that this inability is revealed to the seller and perhaps to other customers. Thus, the audience may be real or presumed (ibid.). Though the other customers may not even notice the problem with the credit card, the cardholder is very likely to feel uneasy and at the centre of attention.

As pointed out by Dahl et al. (2001), embarrassment can involve all phases of purchasing and consumption: one can feel this emotion when making a purchase, for example, when taking a pack of condoms from the display or paying for them. The moment of consumption can be embarrassing, such as dining at a sophisticated restaurant in jeans or being discovered smoking in the toilet of a plane. The post-consumption phase, for example, returning an adult film, may also be tinged by this emotion. Embarrassment is an emotion sometimes used by advertisers to attract the attention of a distracted spectator (and potential customer), as shown in Box 3.2.

Marketing managers may be interested in eliciting this emotion in advance and associating it with the failure to use a product or service. One example of this is the *Financial Times* advertisement that contained the headline 'No FT, no comment', reminding the potential reader of how embarrassing it can be to ignore what is going on in the world (O'Shaughnessy and O'Shaughnessy, 2003).

Then there are products that allow consumers to prevent this emotion, such as mouthwash for fighting bad breath or adhesives for false teeth. Lau-Gesk and Drolet (2008) analyse the effectiveness of two communication methods used to promote this type of product:

BOX 3.2   DOES TRASH IN ADVERTISING WORK? DISGUST AND EMBARRASSMENT USED TO ATTRACT ATTENTION

The 2005 Dolce & Gabbana advertisement for watches created by two fashion designers aroused much debate among viewers and advertising experts. Many considered the commercial to be of dubious taste, if not downright disgusting. The commercial shows two young people exchanging gifts after a romantic dinner. The man gives the woman a Dolce & Gabbana watch. At this point she passes wind, an event that embarrasses not just the woman but also the astonished viewer. The loving companion stops her embarrassment immediately by exceeding her performance with an even more powerful emission. Dolce & Gabbana narrate, in a questionable and curious manner, that there can be no inhibitions in love: the claim '*For real lovers*' supports this interpretation. If the objective of its creators was to ensure that the commercial attracted people's attention and made them remember it, it was successful: even the most distracted viewer could not have ignored the communication. If, on the other hand, the aim was to create brand attraction and therefore to affect the behaviour of potential purchasers, the idea may not have been successful: it naturally depends on the taste and sensitivity of the target audience. These doubts regarding the real effectiveness of trash, however, do not seem to affect Italian marketing managers, who have always used this kind of advertising. One example is Oliviero Toscani and his Benetton posters: who among us has forgotten the posters of the baby with its umbilical cord still attached or the kiss between a priest and a nun?

Source: Addis and Soscia (2006).

the advertising message can highlight the consequences of non-use or the benefits of use. The scholars demonstrate how only the first type of appeal is effective when the public comprises people with limited *public self-consciousness* and thus a low inclination to experience embarrassment. The purchase of products designed to prevent embarrassment can, however, be an embarrassing experience in itself. In this regard, Dahl et al. (2001) point out how marketing managers should promote self-service in stores to limit this negative emotion: forcing customers to ask the chemist for a box of condoms or a pregnancy test – as opposed to allowing people to take them off a shelf themselves – certainly does not boost sales of these products.

Table 3.4 shows the consumer appraisals, appraisals acting, the tactics used by marketing managers and the consumer action tendencies considered above.

3.4 PRIDE: COGNITIVE ANTECEDENTS AND ACTION TENDENCIES

Pride is a social emotion of positive value. The two main cognitive antecedents of this emotion are achieving a goal or a positive result, and attributing that success to oneself rather than to other people or to chance (Mascolo and Fischer, 1995; Roseman et al., 1996; Bagozzi, 1999). Kant used an interesting metaphor to distinguish the various *appraisals* of happiness and pride, underlining how each of us can taste a superbly prepared dish with pleasure, but only the chef can feel proud of the result (Weiner, 1985, p. 561).

Pride is often elicited by a comparative appraisal (Mascolo and Fischer, 1995), in the sense that Kant's chef will feel particularly proud if she is aware that she is one of the few people capable of cooking that dish successfully. The comparative element highlights an interesting characteristic of this emotion: even if pride derives from reflection on oneself, the judgement of other people is of crucial importance. Moreover, the connection with the self can reflect various levels of abstraction: we feel proud when we consider ourselves somehow responsible for a positive result, for example when the football team we play in wins a tournament, but we also feel this emotion when we are near or connected to a successful person. For example, we are also proud when the football team we support wins.

*Table 3.4   Consumer shame and embarrassment: appraisals,
actions triggered by appraisals, marketing tactics, action
tendencies*

Shame/Embarrassment

Appraisals	Actions triggered by appraisals	Tactic	Action tendencies
Violation of a moral/ social rule	Acting the violation (shame-increasing appeal)	Eliciting anticipated shame with advertisements showing the shameful effect of alcohol abuse	Intention to commit the violation is weakened
	Acting the violation (shame-decreasing appeal)	Decreasing anticipated shame related to the purchase of a sensitive product (e.g., condoms) by portraying it in advertising as 'socially correct and desirable'	Intention to buy is reinforced
Presence of an audience	Acting the presence by emphasizing it	Eliciting anticipated embarrassment with advertisements showing the blame and commiseration of friends of the alcohol abuser	Intention to commit the violation is weakened
	Acting the presence by eliminating it	Decreasing anticipated embarrassment related to the purchase of a sensitive product (e.g., condoms) by providing a self-service option	Intention to buy is reinforced

The typical action tendencies associated with pride are self-celebration and drawing other people's attention to the success in order to ensure that it is recognized and appreciated (Mascolo and Fischer, 1995). Pride is considered a social emotion precisely because of this quest for other people's approval: the experience of pride reflects the advantage that arises from adhering to imposed or internalized

Table 3.5   Pride: cognitive antecedents and action tendencies

Appraisals	Action tendencies
Desirability and causation, specifically: achieving a goal or a positive result and the attribution of that success to oneself	Exuberance Excitement

social standards and rules. This awareness subsequently implies the tendency to repeat actions or behaviours that have led to good results in order to enjoy the sense of self-effectiveness once again and to reinforce the positive opinions of other people. Table 3.5 shows the cognitive antecedents and action tendencies linked to pride.

A close cousin to pride is hubris: both are self-conscious emotions, both are pleasurable emotions, and both occur in response to various instances of personal success (Ruvio and Bagozzi, 2011). Nevertheless, while pride is based on actual success and is metaphorically expressed by the statement 'I'm proud of what I did or I achieved', hubris is based on a distorted view of the self and conveys the thought 'I'm proud of the superior person I am' (Ruvio and Bagozzi, 2011). Thus, while the proud person relates his or her achievements to personal efforts (I succeeded because I worked hard), the hubristic person attributes their success to ability ('I succeeded because I am the best'). Both pride and hubris have been neglected by consumer research despite their important managerial implications, which are discussed in the next section.

3.5   PRIDE AND CONSUMER BEHAVIOUR

Pride, like the other social emotions examined here, can also affect all phases of the product purchase and consumption process. As discussed above, guilt and shame are negative emotions, but they do not necessarily have a negative effect on this process (e.g., they promote contributions to social campaigns). Similarly, pride is not always a desirable emotion, at least from the marketing manager's point of view. For example, anticipated pride may represent a threat to product managers placed in charge of guilty pleasures: Patrick et al. (2009) find that when consumers are exposed to a tempting stimulus, anticipated pride is more effective than anticipated shame in facilitating thoughts and behaviours related to self-control. The authors also demonstrate the process mechanism underlying this effect, explaining that its superior efficacy is due to the attentional focus each anticipated emotion evokes: anticipated shame focuses on the guilty pleasure, while anticipated pride focuses attention on the self. The idea is that distracting attention away from the temptation and toward other stimuli may decrease the desire to succumb to temptation (ibid.).

As we will see, pride can play a decisive role in the phase of perceiving needs and collecting information; it can also affect the purchase process, determine or inhibit repurchase intentions and characterize the consumption experience. With reference to the first phases concerning the sphere of motivation and perception, Aaker and Lee (2001) demonstrate how different advertising appeals, that is, communications expressing different emotions, arouse different degrees of interest and appreciation depending on the reference culture. For example, in contexts such as the Chinese culture, where pride is an emotion that is inhibited from a very early age and where personal success reflects positively on the honour of the institutions to which the person belongs more than on the person him or herself, the communicational appeals that express this emotion are appreciated, as they represent something unusual, something outside the norm. In contrast, this communicational key arouses less attention and curiosity in individualistic cultures such as the one prevalent in the USA, where self-esteem is considered an indispensable requirement for success and where the pursuit of individual happiness prevails over the pursuit of social well-being. In the latter type of culture, in fact, pride is an advertising appeal that evokes memories of well-known, routine situations and experiences (Aaker and Lee, 2001). In this regard, these findings are in line with Helson's (1959) adaptation-level theory.

With regard to Western societies, hubris perceived in others (e.g., a hubristic testimonial in advertising) has been shown to generate more positive evaluations of products and a higher willingness to buy than pride does (Ruvio and Bagozzi, 2011). The authors maintain that the observation of people who express hubris in conjunction with the possession of a product will induce non-owners to carry out a social comparison and to arrive at a positive evaluation of a product capable of enhancing her status and power (ibid.).

Pride can also affect the moment of purchase. In this context, marketing scholars investigating the success of discount coupons compared to other forms of promotion (e.g., a discount of equivalent value) have tested the role played by pride in the preference of consumers for this particular type of incentive. In this vein, Babakus et al. (1988) analyse the reasons for using discount coupons. As in other types of promotions, the users of these coupons are characterized by greater price sensitivity than the average purchaser, but they attribute less value to time (again in comparison to the average): looking for, selecting and collecting discount coupons, and collecting points are very often time-consuming activities, but those who take advantage of such promotions do not feel that their energy is wasted. The third motive underlying the use of discount coupons is the pride that one feels during this process of collection and use, or 'the good feelings that result from having done something good' (Babakus et al., 1988, p. 39). In the cognitive antecedents of pride, the authors therefore identify the assumptions examined above, namely the success of coupons compared to a discount of the same value: those who use a discount coupon do not feel proud for having obtained an advantage, but for having worked hard to obtain it.

Pride can also characterize a particular brand. In this context, Gladden and Funk (2002) reconstructed the means–end chains of sports teams, such as Milan and Juventus in soccer, thus establishing the connections between attributes, benefits and values characterizing this very special product category. In particular, the authors discovered that *pride of place*, that is, the ability of a sports team to fittingly represent the town to which it belongs and to lend prestige to a certain community or geographical area through its successes, is an important brand attribute. We can thus imagine that this emotion can also positively characterize the brands sponsoring these teams.

Pride can also reflect negatively on consumer behaviour. In some cases, for example, it can inhibit repurchases (Louro et al., 2005). In the regulatory focus theory formulated by Higgins (2002), the author classifies pride into two categories: *promotion pride* elicited by an awareness of having achieved a positive result thanks to one's efforts and abilities, and *prevention pride*, which instead derives from the knowledge of having avoided a failure. As highlighted in the first chapter, the cognitive elaboration of a certain stimulus is character-

Table 3.6   Consumer pride: appraisals, actions triggered by appraisals, marketing tactics, action tendencies

Pride

Appraisals	Actions triggered by appraisals	Tactic	Action tendencies
Goal achievement and self-responsibility	Acting the goal achievement and self-responsibility (pride-increasing appeal)	Eliciting anticipated pride with social campaigns showing a perfect physical shape obtained by a proper diet	Self-control is reinforced

ized by a strong subjective component. Therefore, given a certain consumption experience and bearing in mind the subjective component that characterizes its interpretation, some consumers will be more willing to experience prevention pride, while others will be more inclined to experience promotion pride. For example, let us try to live out a purchase experience that each reader, or at least the less timid and more presumptuous ones, will have certainly experienced at least once in their lives. Let us put ourselves in the shoes of a consumer who has managed to purchase a product at a particularly interesting price thanks to her negotiating skills. When the customer makes a purchase at the desired price, she may experience promotion pride or prevention pride depending on her subjective inclination. The consumer who experiences promotion pride feels proud of having got a good deal, while the customer experiences prevention pride in having avoided purchasing the product at its full price. Louro et al. (2005) demonstrate how the latter type of customer – wary, suspicious and diffident by nature – is not very inclined to repurchase from the same seller or provider, while the former wishes to relive the same positive emotion by making subsequent purchases from the same supplier.

Finally, passionate expressions of national pride may also lead to consumer prejudices toward foreign brands and attachment to domestic products (e.g., Wang, 2006; Wang and Wang, 2007). Table 3.6 presents examples of pride management, while Table 3.7 examines the role of these social emotions during the various phases of the purchase and consumption process.

Table 3.7 Social emotions during the various phases of the purchase and consumption process

Phases of the purchase and consumption process	Social emotions		
	Sense of guilt	Shame and embarrassment	Pride
		EXAMPLES	
Perception of need, search for information and assessment of alternatives	Anticipated guilt can be a communicational appeal capable of directing preferences towards a particular charity (e.g., Un Techo para Chile campaign)	Shock appeal, that is, a type of communication capable of embarrassing a potential customer, can be used to attract attention	Pride is an advertising lever that can arouse the target's interest in the advertisement and the communicated product
Moment of purchase	Making an important purchase without informing and involving the family can generate guilt	The purchase of *sensitive* products from a chemist, such as condoms or laxatives, may be embarrassing	Taking advantage of particular types of promotions, such as collecting and using discount coupons, can instil pride

76

Moment of consumption	The gift-with-purchase promotion may relieve guilt when, for example, the gift is meant to be enjoyed by someone else. Consumption of a *guilty pleasure*, such as a cake, can generate a sense of guilt	Embarrassment can derive from a sense of inappropriateness during the use of a service, such as dining in a luxury restaurant in casual attire. Failure to consume a certain product, such as a deodorant, can be embarrassing	*Pride of place* is a typical consumption emotion elicited by the successes of the team one supports
Post-consumption phase	Regret may induce return of products	Interaction with the service provider and with the other customers, such as having an audience when returning an adult film, can sometimes be embarrassing	*Promotion pride*, but not *prevention pride*, can positively affect repurchase intentions

4. Anger and gratitude

After analysing the emotions deriving from fortunate and unfortunate events (Chapter 2) and from those we are responsible for (Chapter 3), we shall now concentrate on the emotive states originating from other people's actions. In particular, we shall focus on anger, which is elicited by *appraisals* of a negative event caused by third parties, and on gratitude, its specular positive emotion. Anger and gratitude have been studied in cognitive psychology, and some of the conclusions drawn in this area are certainly of interest for the purchase and consumption processes as well.

4.1 ANGER: COGNITIVE ANTECEDENTS AND ACTION TENDENCIES

In psychological literature, anger is considered an emotive reaction to an adverse state (Canary and Semic, 1999). In the light of this characterization, we can say that this emotion is distinguished by the antecedent of desirability (or non-desirability). According to these authors, causation is the second important antecedent of anger. In fact, when our existence is affected by a negative event, we instinctively attempt to identify responsibility, and as soon as we identify it in an external agent, the emotion we feel is anger (Izard, 1991; Lazarus, 1991; Clore et al., 1993).

More precisely, we get angry with people who offend us when we feel that the negative behaviour could somehow be controlled by the external agent (Canary and Semic, 1999), when we are intentionally offended, or when we are harmed by a person's negligence (Ben-Ze'ev, 2000). For example, a shop assistant who does not immediately pay attention to us because she is busy with another customer can induce a state of frustration in us, while one who neglects us because she is involved in a long and frivolous personal telephone conversation can make us angry (Lazarus, 1991).

Table 4.1   *Anger: cognitive antecedents and action tendencies*

	Cognitive antecedents	Action tendencies

Anger	Non-desirability
	External agent responsibility
	Ability to prevent the negative
	   outcome
		Confrontive coping, reaction,
		   antagonism

Therefore, like hate and disgust, anger implies a negative evaluation. However, unlike the other two emotions, the negative evaluation leading to anger relates to a specific action and not to the person in the overall sense (Ben-Ze'ev, 2000): the irritating sales assistant mentioned above will therefore be the object of our anger rather than of our hatred.

As regards the type of behaviour aroused in us, anger mobilizes the energies required to 'respond to the attack' (Izard, 1991): 'the urge to attack is essential to anger, even if it is expressed in non-aggressive behaviour' (Ben-Ze'ev, 2000, p. 384). Frijda et al. (1989) associates this emotion with the action tendencies of 'reaction' and 'antagonism' (Table 4.1).

In this sense, it is interesting to see how anger, unlike hatred, involves the idea that the negative situation is potentially reversible. The problem that makes us angry could be solved (Ben-Ze'ev, 2000). For example, the irritating sales assistant who captures our angry glances can rapidly put down the phone and serve us, thus neutralizing a potential situation of conflict. This emotion therefore implies the possibility of communication, which is expressed in nonverbal form in the example above. Paradoxically, anger suggests a cooperative approach, the effort to understand the other person's point of view, and a potential acceptance of responsibility (Canary and Semic, 1999). According to Stearns (1972), anger can only be aroused in affectively mature people, while hatred is an indicator of immaturity.

In the light of these considerations, when anger is not pathologically characterized, it becomes a very powerful tool for preserving a relationship. Generally speaking, an angry individual intends to restore a spoiled relationship by genuinely expressing her disappointment (Izard, 1991). Therefore, as can be readily imagined, the correct management of an angry customer is a question of vital importance for the marketing manager. This will become even more evident below.

However, it is important to point out that anger is also very frequently expressed due to an incorrect attribution of responsibility. We also get angry when the error is ours, as the tendency not to accept responsibility is part of human nature: 'people often try to find someone or something to blame, which makes anger a very frequent emotion, even under ambiguous conditions, as long as the victim of a slight can find a scapegoat' (Lazarus, 1991, p. 224). The marketing implications of this assiduous quest for a scapegoat can be rather serious. On the one hand, the customer is not always right, and it is not so simple to enlighten them in this respect. On the other hand, producers and service providers are not always willing to admit their shortcomings and therefore 'accept' the consumer's anger.

4.2   ANGER AND CONSUMER BEHAVIOUR

Consumer anger is defined by Funches (2011, p. 421) as an emotional state that stems from a consumer's perceived loss of entitlement due to an unfair, threatening or harmful consumption experience. As the hedonic bias drives consumers to ascribe failures to others rather than to themselves, anger rather than guilt is considered the prevalent affective reaction to product and service failures (Gelbrich, 2010).

Funches (2011) identifies three possible causes of consumer anger: broken promises, unfair treatment and expressed hostility. The first cause may arise in the case of a company that promises a money-back guarantee and then refuses to deliver on that promise. The second involves situations that favour the company excessively (e.g., an overly strict returns policy), while the third reflects the consumer's belief that someone at the company expressed hostility towards them (e.g., an impolite sales assistant).

Most of the time, disservices elicit both anger and dissatisfaction. We get angry and dissatisfied when we wait too long for a service, when we interact with an inattentive sales assistant, when we see an error on a receipt, and so on. However, as discussed in Chapter 2 and in the previous section, anger and dissatisfaction are characterized by different action tendencies. In the light of the psychological literature examined, we can suppose that an angry consumer will be more inclined to complain than a dissatisfied one. The marketing implications of these two emotional experiences are therefore very different: unlike mere dissatisfaction, the consumer's anger would allow the firm to respond to the complaint adequately and thus to restore the trust of a consumer who threatens to terminate her relationship with the brand. Given these important implications, Bougie et al. (2003) analysed this distinction in detail.

First of all, the scholars investigated whether the two emotions exhibit a different experiential profile in the sphere of demand analysis. In order to do so, the authors conducted a descriptive study involving 120 subjects. Half the sample was asked to recall an experience with a *service provider* that made them angry, while the other half was asked to recollect an experience of using a service that left them dissatisfied. The services mentioned by the respondents were varied. They referred to transport (e.g., trains, buses, planes and taxis), telecommunications, distribution and restaurant services, schools, banks and insurance companies, travel agents and so on.

It emerged that the two consumption emotions feature different sensations and reflections. The angry consumer 'feels he is exploding' and has the impression of being overcome by his emotions; he broods over the wrong he has suffered and has violent thoughts. The customer would therefore like to react aggressively and complain, and at times he may make unpleasant and angry remarks. Anger induces him to confront the service provider and, in extreme cases, to offend her. The ultimate objective of this aggressive behaviour is to dissuade the provider from repeating her incorrect behaviour and, above all, to obtain compensation. The dissatisfied customer, on the other hand, is pervaded by a sense of failed satisfaction; he wonders what went wrong and how to address the situation.

The identification of two separate experiential profiles is of interest for the marketing manager. In fact, although the two emotions seem to be related in some circumstances, there may be other purchase or consumption situations in which the customer is simply dissatisfied or simply angry. As the tendencies to action arising from these two emotions are very different, this distinction is a crucial one.

In a second study, Bougie et al. (2003) set out to correlate the two emotions with types of post-purchase behaviour of interest for marketing managers. In particular, the authors examined complaints to the provider, complaints made to third parties (e.g., consumer associations), negative word of mouth and abandonment in favour of another service provider.

The collected data demonstrates that, unlike anger, dissatisfaction does not directly generate complaints and negative word of mouth. The latter phenomenon is a particularly harmful form of post-consumption behaviour because it produces negative attitudes in other customers and prevents them from buying the products or using the services of a specific company. Anger completely mediates the relationship between dissatisfaction and these actions, while it only partially mediates the relationship between dissatisfaction and abandonment. In line with the psychological literature examined above, these conclusions highlight how the emotion of dissatisfaction is potentially more dangerous to the service provider. Some disappointed customers will terminate the relationship without attempting to argue their point of view, that is, without giving the service provider the opportunity to restore the relationship.

Nevertheless, according to Beverland et al. (2010), when consumers frame conflicts in *personal terms*, post-conflict relations often result in an angry exit. This may stem from the expressed hostility mentioned above. In such situations, the negative outcome arises even if a good level of service recovery is implemented (Beverland et al., 2010). This is not the case in *task conflicts*, where consumers are more focused on the material aspects of the disservice. When a service failure is framed in these terms, consumers are more receptive to genuine efforts at service recovery (ibid.).

Therefore, managing angry consumers is a strategic activity for the enterprise, as is demonstrated by the numerous training initiatives specifically designed to instruct the sales force in this area.[1] It is also important to consider the fact that unsuitable reactions to customer anger can lead to truly furious reactions (Bonifield and Cole, 2007).

In a study based on a *content analysis* of 299 reports published on the web by consumers who narrate their experience of a restaurant service, Bonifield and Cole (ibid.) classified the possible reactions of restaurateurs to customer anger and the post-purchase behaviour exhibited by the customer in response to those reactions (see Table 4.2).

Research has demonstrated that aggravating action makes customers angry and causes them to exhibit retaliatory behaviour without reserve. On the other hand, it seems that behaviour aimed

Table 4.2 *Possible reactions to customer anger and the resulting post-purchase behaviour*

Type	Behaviour	Example
Customer 'revenge'	Aggressive complaint	'... at that point my wife got up, looked the manager in the eye and gave it to him ...'
	Narration of the experience	'... I told my friends what had happened ...'
	Negative publicity	'... I advised all my friends and colleagues to keep away from that restaurant ...'
'Conciliatory' response of the customer	Rebate	'... I asked for my money back ...'
	Suggesting an improvement	'... they should increase the staff to reduce the service times ...'
	Positive word of mouth	'I will probably recommend it to my friends'
	Certain repurchase	'We'll be back on Friday evening'
	Probable repurchase	'I'd like to try their brunch ...'
Action taken by the service provider to appease the customer	The 'It could have been worse' strategy	'Just imagine ... it was even worse at lunchtime: given the problems we've had in the kitchen, our customers had to wait up to an hour before being served ...'
	Excuses	'... the cook came and apologized ...'
Aggravating actions taken by the service provider	Attempt to place the blame for the disservice on the customer	'I had asked for some biscuits and jam but someone had spread butter on them. When I pointed out the error, the waiter, lying, told me that I had ordered them with butter'
	Rude behaviour	'An outburst like that can ruin the whole day!'

Source: Adapted from Bonfield and Cole (2007).

at appeasing the consumer's anger, despite being unable to neutralize this emotion, can generate profitable conciliatory responses. In
this regard, it may be useful if the excuses quoted by Bonifield and
Cole (2007) include a *retrospective explanation*, namely why a failure
occurred (see Box 4.1) and/or why the organization could not avoid
it.

According to Gelbrich (2010), retrospective explanation is an
effective marketing tool. It may help customers to re-evaluate a
problem as less severe, initiating positive reappraisals and decreasing anger. In fact, learning about JetBlue Airways' view of failure
(Box 4.1) helps empathetic consumers to understand the company's
position. The exceptionally adverse circumstances may help consumers to understand the company's position and mitigate their anger.

Unfortunately, it is not easy to prevent 'aggravating behaviour'
on the part of the service provider. In order to fully understand this
difficulty, we can simply return to the emotive contagion theory
described in Chapter 2. In this context, Dallimore et al. (2007)
demonstrate that when an angry consumer complains, she triggers a process of emotional contagion that 'infects' the seller and
negatively affects their mood and behaviour. In fact, when a shop
assistant is attacked by the action of *complaining*, she unknowingly
tends to display uncontrolled, non-verbal negative behaviour. They
may open their eyes wide, attempt to avoid the customer's gaze, put
on a forced smile or a sullen stare, fail to control their expressions of
disapproval, bite their lip, and so on. The customer perceives these
signals, and this type of behaviour obviously exacerbates the tension
in the relationship, thus generating a negative emotive spiral. Only
suitable staff training activities can alter our natural tendency to
respond violently and defensively to aggression, even if it is motivated and legitimate. Moreover, because customers frequently do
not voice their anger to service providers, it is important for the
employees to ask customers for their opinions in order to be able
to adapt the service. Thus, actively listening to customers instead
of just selling the product is a fundamental aspect to bear in mind
when managing customer anger (Sanchez-Garcia and Curras-Perez,
2011).

A company might also reduce the likelihood of customer anger
by improving service quality and promising only what it can actually deliver (ibid.). In this regard, the firm can clarify its positioning
by recourse to *prospective explanation*. The company can anticipate

BOX 4.1   AN APOLOGY FROM JETBLUE AIRWAYS

Dear JetBlue Customers,
We are sorry and embarrassed. But most of all, we are deeply sorry.

Last week was the worst operational week in JetBlue's seven-year history. Following the severe winter ice storm in the Northeast, we subjected our customers to unacceptable delays, flight cancellations, lost baggage, and other major inconveniences. The storm disrupted the movement of aircraft, and, more importantly, disrupted the movement of JetBlue's pilot and inflight crewmembers who were depending on those planes to get them to the airports where they were scheduled to serve you. With the busy President's Day weekend upon us, rebooking opportunities were scarce and hold times at 1-800-JETBLUE were unacceptably long or not even available, further hindering our recovery efforts.

Words cannot express how truly sorry we are for the anxiety, frustration and inconvenience that we caused. This is especially saddening because JetBlue was founded on the promise of bringing humanity back to air travel and making the experience of flying happier and easier for everyone who chooses to fly with us. We know we failed to deliver on this promise last week.

We are committed to you, our valued customers, and are taking immediate corrective steps to regain your confidence in us. We have begun putting a comprehensive plan in place to provide better and more timely information to you, more tools and resources for our crewmembers and improved procedures for handling operational difficulties in the future. We are confident, as a result of these actions, that JetBlue will emerge as a more reliable and even more customer responsive airline than ever before.

Most importantly, we have published the JetBlue Airways Customer Bill of Rights – our official commitment to you of how we will handle operational interruptions going forward – including details of compensation.

> You deserved better – a lot better – from us last week. Nothing is more important than regaining your trust and all of us here hope you will give us the opportunity to welcome you onboard again soon and provide you the positive JetBlue Experience you have come to expect from us.
>
> Sincerely,
> David Neeleman
> Founder and CEO
> JetBlue Airways
>
> *Source:* Personal communication.

possible future problems with the service and explain why they are unavoidable and/or beyond the company's control. Prospective explanations serve to mitigate the problem of helplessness, which in turn moderates the relationship between anger and vindictive, negative word of mouth (Gelbrich, 2010).

Another way to reduce the likelihood of consumer anger is to help consumers perform a careful attributional appraisal (Soscia, 2007). Unfortunately, from the firm's point of view, consumers sometimes do not perform this appraisal correctly. Although consumers may feel confident about their inferences, their perceived reasons may differ from the 'true' reasons for service/product failure. This possibility may have prompted British Airways in 2001 to publish new rules for passengers asserting that the airline can bar them from boarding its aircraft if they appear abusive, insulting, threatening or disorderly in any way (O'Shaughnessy and O'Shaughnessy, 2003).

Managers at British Airways wished to prevent damaging or incorrect attributions; to this end, they emphasized the fact that there are particular situations in which service can be denied to consumers who act inappropriately. Managers can facilitate consumers' causal attributions in a number of ways. For example, as in the case of British Airways, they can use the communication mix to clarify the roles that consumers should play in the consumption, delivery and administration of a particular product or service. If they wish to be effective, marketers should communicate the expected role of consumers in a very clear, precise, respectful and honest way,

without relieving the company of its responsibilities and preroga-
tives. However, this apparently was not the case at British Airways.
According to O'Shaughnessy and O'Shaughnessy (2003), the rules
that British Airways promulgated were vague and ambiguous, with
too much left to the consumer's discretion: 'there is the need to
explicate the relevant behavior through thick description and videos
illustrating the banned behavior' (ibid., p. 19). In any case, it appears
that the managers at British Airways were right in concluding that
consumers do not always form correct attributions of negative
outcomes.

Sometimes uncertainty arises, for example when a product is
complex (Folkes, 1984). Therefore, companies should do their best
to facilitate consumer attributions, and there are various ways to
induce consumers to recognize and accept responsibility if they are,
in fact, responsible for negative outcomes. For example, companies
can do so by advising consumers to take specific precautions in
using a particular product. In a co-advertising campaign in Italy,
Benetton recommends using a specific detergent to protect clothes
from fading. In general, advertising and other communications
should convey frank messages that do not minimize the commitment consumers are expected to make in order to obtain benefits
from a service or a product. Marketing managers should also take
advantage of other opportunities, such as discussing the reasons
for negative outcomes with their customers. This can be done in
response to letters from consumers requesting product information as well as in situations where consumers return products for
refunds (ibid.). In these cases, manufacturers and service providers
have the chance to inform their customers about possible product
misuse.

Table 4.3 summarizes the consumer appraisals, actions triggered
by appraisals, the tactics used by marketing managers and the
consumers' action tendencies discussed above.

While the discussion about anger has thus far focused on dis-
satisfying relationships between customers and companies, Porath
et al. (2010) remind us that customers are also likely to regard
uncivilized episodes between employees as unpleasant, and that such
episodes damage the perceived quality of service. Whereas incivility
directed at customers makes them angry (see above), Porath et al.
(ibid.) showed that customers are also negatively affected when they
witness incivility between employees. These conflicts are deleterious

Table 4.3 Consumer anger: appraisals, actions triggered by appraisals, marketing tactics, action tendencies

Anger

Appraisals	Actions triggered by appraisals	Tactic	Action tendencies
Non-desirability	Acting the non-desirability, putting the event back into perspective	'It could have been worse' tactic	Conciliatory responses such as suggesting an improvement
Producer/service provider responsibility	Re-appraising responsibility	Excuses with a retrospective explanation (why the problem or disservice occurred). See, for example, the exceptionally severe ice storm quoted by JetBlue (Box 4.1)	Prevention of negative word of mouth and vindictive complaining
		Excuses with a prospective explanation (why the problem or disservice will occur). One example is this message from SouthAir (Iceland): 'SouthAir is currently relocating within the Keflavik Airport area. For this reason we apologize for any disturbance this may cause our clients today and tomorrow.	

	We look forward to meeting you at our new location, which will be announced as soon as we've moved'
	Informing customers about possible product misuse: for example, Benetton recommends using a specific detergent to protect clothes from fading
Ability to prevent the negative outcome	Excuses with a retrospective explanation (why the organization could not avoid the problem or disservice). For example, the JetBlue crewmembers who were supposed to serve delayed customers also fell victim to delays themselves (see Box 4.1)
	Excuses with a prospective explanation (why the organization will not be able to avoid the problem or disservice)

to companies because they elicit consumer anger, causing customers to make negative generalizations that affect their judgement of the company as a whole (ibid.). Curiously, incivility elicits negative reactions only when customers observe employee–employee arguments, while customer incivility towards an employee does not bring about the same effect (ibid.).

We end this section with one possible positive effect of anger on consumer behaviour. In this regard, Veling et al. (2011) studied the positive effects that arise from associating anger with a product, demonstrating that anger conveyed through a product enhances the desire for and value of that product when it is perceived as attainable. This may be the case with Lion candy bars (ibid.), where the angry lion associated with the bars motivates people to buy them. According to those scholars, 'anger, through its approach-related nature, may amplify the extent to which the object then turns into a reward that motivates people to invest resources (e.g., efforts or money) to obtain it' (ibid.).

4.3 GRATITUDE: COGNITIVE ANTECEDENTS AND TENDENCIES TO ACTION

Just as anger is close to hate (given that both derive from the negative evaluation of an external agent), gratitude is similar to love because both imply a positive judgement from a cognitive standpoint. Unlike love and hate, however, anger and gratitude do not focus on a person, but rather on an action performed by a person (Ben-Ze'ev, 2000).

Numerous authors consider gratitude to be an emotive trait rather than an emotion. Most psychologists have focused their studies on grateful people rather than on the individual emotions associated with this state. Generally speaking, the terms 'gratitude', 'grateful' and 'thankful' are rarely mentioned by psychologists studying emotions (McCullough et al., 2001). Moreover, despite its relevance, gratitude seems difficult to experience. It is certainly experienced far less frequently than the other positive emotions. A study conducted on American and German adults, for example, shows that a mere 10 per cent frequently have outbursts of gratitude. Moreover, just 20 per cent of the interviewees recognize a social or adaptive function in this state (ibid.).

Table 4.4 Gratitude: cognitive antecedents and action tendencies

	Cognitive antecedents	Action tendencies
Gratitude	Desirability External agent responsibility	Approach

The cognitivists McCullough et al. (2004, p. 295) define gratitude as an empathetic emotion that reflects recognition and appreciation of an altruistic gesture. Experiencing a sense of gratitude is different from feeling in debt: 'gratitude does not lead to mindless tit-for-tat behavior' (Fredrickson, 2004, p. 150). Grateful people cannot wait to reward their benefactors, while 'debtors' tend to avoid them (McCullough et al., 2004). In the light of this definition, it thus seems that, as in the case of anger, the two cognitive antecedents of this emotion are desirability and causation (see Table 4.4).

This state is clearly classified among the positive emotions (Fredrickson, 2004) and is generated when a subject attributes a positive *outcome* to the generosity of a benefactor who expressly acted in the interest of the beneficiary (McCullough et al., 2001; Fredrickson, 2004). According to McCullough et al. (2001), the intentional action of the benefactor is just one of the three conditions that promote a feeling of gratitude. The other two are the effective success of this action, meaning that mere good intentions on the part of the benefactor are insufficient, and the capacity of the benefactor to accept the beneficiary's gratitude.

Although these are relevant conditions, they are not completely necessary in order to elicit a sense of gratitude (ibid.), unlike the two basic cognitive antecedents suggested above. In fact, nearly all of us have at least once been grateful to people who have worked for us with the best intentions but without achieving any success. We may even be grateful to a cat who keeps us company on a rainy and sad day without the cat necessarily grasping our emotion empathetically.

With reference to action tendencies, gratitude extends the cognitive possibilities (as do the other positive emotions), while negative emotions induce focalization (Fredrickson, 2004). In particular, gratitude induces pro-social behaviour towards both the benefactor and the community in general. It is therefore a state that elicits altruistic reactions, behaviour that strengthens friendship, alliances and social ties in general: 'gratitude serves to link individual to society' (ibid., p. 151).

In the light of the functionalist perspective discussed in Chapter 1, we can identify three important functions of this emotion (McCullogh et al., 2001):

- *Moral barometer function.* A barometer is a tool that reflects a change with respect to a previous state (e.g., a change in weather). Gratitude 'informs' us of the fact that we have benefited from someone else and that the actions of our benefactor have improved our existential state. This emotion therefore measures positive interpersonal input.
- *Moral stimulus function.* In grateful people, this emotion is able to stimulate pro-social actions: gratitude is, in fact, considered to be one of the possible motivational mechanisms lying at the basis of altruism.
- *Moral support function.* The expression of the beneficiary's gratitude towards the benefactor strengthens the altruistic impulse of the latter, who will be even more motivated to exhibit such benevolence in future. This third function indicates an interesting tie with another positive emotion previously examined: pride. In fact, it would seem that the gratitude of the beneficiary instils pride in the originator of the benevolent action, who is then animated with additional good intentions for the future. Gratitude therefore proves to be a very powerful tool, as it can activate a virtuous circle that could lead us to an increasingly close and united world: the socio-emotional cycle activated by gratitude may continue indefinitely (Fredrickson, 2004, p. 159).

Gratitude is also indissolubly connected with states of happiness (Watkins, 2004). In fact, thanking people is not a mere expression of gratitude to those who have given us joy, but it is above all the necessary coronation of a state of contentment, the fulfilment of a happy moment: 'The test of all happiness is gratitude' (Chesterton, 1986, quoted in Watkins, 2004, p. 167).

The economic implications of the latter considerations warrant attentive reflection. It seems that organizations whose employees feel this triad of emotions are distinguished by low *turnover*, greater customer loyalty and higher revenues and profits (Fredrickson, 2004, p. 159).

4.4 GRATITUDE AND CONSUMER BEHAVIOUR

Despite its relevant managerial implications, gratitude has been somewhat neglected not only in psychological studies, but also in marketing studies. As we have seen, however, people still love to reward hard work and commitment. And so does the consumer, at least according Morales (2005) and Palmatier et al. (2009). This is especially evident in charitable giving, where this emotion, among other possible explanations (e.g., self-esteem, tax or career motives), is the best predictor of monetary giving to medical charities (Dawson, 1988).

Many marketing researchers also point out the importance of the principle of reciprocity, but 'neither of these approaches offers insight into the potentially important underlying causal element of gratitude, which may be responsible, at least in part, for the observed reciprocating behaviors' (Palmatier et al., 2009, p. 2).

Palmatier et al. (2009) demonstrate that gratitude mediates the impact of a seller's relationship marketing investments on performance outcomes such as purchase intentions, share of wallet, sales revenues and sales growth, beyond the contributions of trust and commitment. Thus gratitude plays an important mediating role beyond the contributions of trust and commitment. According to Morales (2005), these marketing investments should be conceived as forms of extra commitment. The scholar classifies these extra commitments into two types: efforts designed to benefit the individual customer and efforts that set out to reward and delight the community of consumers.

The first class includes, for example, the care and attention a sales assistant devotes to a customer who purchases a garment; at that moment, the former may become a passionate *personal shopper* instead of a mere sales assistant. This dedication, which is highly appreciated by the author, is becoming increasingly rare in a world of clothing dominated by mass distribution, but according to Morales (2005) it is welcomed with gratitude as well as a sense of indebtedness.

One example that can be placed in the second category is the work done by a distributor in the radical reorganization of category management in order to help the customer choose among various commercial offers. It is, in fact, an activity aimed to optimize decision-making for all customers, not just for the individual consumer. In this case, the purchaser will be grateful to the distributor, but without feeling indebted to the latter.

Morales (ibid.) has empirically demonstrated that in both cases the consumer, animated by a sense of gratitude, will be prompted to 'reward' the producer or service provider with a greater inclination to spend. This action tendency is similar to those indicated in the psychological literature discussed in the previous section. In the final chapter, we will see that a sense of gratitude can elicit other types of post-purchase behaviours that are favourable to the firm.

Lastly, the author highlights how these types of behaviour are only exhibited when the persuasive intention of the company is not declared excessively: 'when firms are thought to be exerting effort with the intent to persuade, consumers no longer respond positively' (Morales, 2005, p. 811). In this regard, Palmatier et al. (2009) suggest that companies leverage relationship marketing investments by developing programmes that enhance customer perceptions of the seller's free will and benevolence when providing benefits. For example, in addition to finding an apartment for a foreign customer, a relocation agency might also offer to help her open a bank account in order to mitigate the typical bureaucratic difficulties people face when they move to another country.

Beyond the strategy discussed above, companies may elicit customer gratitude by providing benefit when the customer's need is the highest and the benefit provides the most perceived value. This may be the case with a hotel that provides the older guests with the most easily accessible rooms. Possible strategies designed to elicit gratitude are shown in Table 4.5.

According to Palmatier et al. (2009), these tactics are effective only if sellers give the client an occasion to reciprocate soon after providing them with extra benefits, 'which takes advantage of high levels of gratitude, prevents guilt rationalizations, and leads to cycles of reciprocation' (ibid., p. 14).

While so far we have analysed only the gratitude that a consumer may feel towards a specific company, it is interesting to note that

Table 4.5   *Consumer gratitude: appraisals, actions triggered by appraisals, marketing tactics, action tendencies*

Gratitude			
Appraisals	Actions triggered by appraisals	Tactic	Action tendencies
Desirability	Acting the desirability, exploiting provided benefits	Providing a benefit when the customer's need is the highest and the benefit provides the most perceived value (e.g., by upgrading an injured customer to first class if there are seats available)	Intention to buy Positive word of mouth
Producer/ service provider responsi- bility	Reappraising responsibility, working on seller's free will and benevolence	Allowing employees more discretion in relationship marketing investments and encouraging extra efforts on the part of employees: for example, the company might provide incentives to employees who stay at work longer in order to assist a customer in need	

expressions of gratitude to customers are abundant in marketing management (Raggio and Garretson Folse, 2009). An example of this practice is shown in Box 4.2, where a pet bird food company writes to thank its clients: they published the message on their website on the occasion of the Thanksgiving holiday.

Raggio and Garretson Folse (ibid.) found that customers who read or hear such thankful advertisements develop a more positive attitude towards the company, show a greater willingness to pay a premium for the appreciative companies' products, and spread positive word of mouth. The scholars also demonstrate that such expressions of gratitude only work when they are perceived as sincere.

Finally, the sense of gratitude felt by customers may also help in the development of a specific line of business (Chan and Li, 2010).

BOX 4.2   A SENTIMENT OF GRATITUDE BY LAFEBER COMPANY

It is Thanksgiving time again and our thoughts turn toward counting our blessings. At Lafeber Company, we are very thankful for all of our customers. We enjoy talking to you about your birds, answering your questions and listening to your suggestions.

WE THANK YOU FOR BEING OUR LOYAL CUSTOMERS!
Naturally, we always give thanks because you purchase our bird food and make us a productive business. We are thrilled that you go to great lengths to order your Lafeber favorites, look for them in pet stores all over the country and call us once in a while to see what is new on the market.

WE THANK YOU FOR BUYING OUR PRODUCTS!
Our most fervent gratitude to each of you goes far beyond sales and is truly a sincere appreciation for sharing our passion – you care about the health and happiness of your birds. You choose to feed Lafeber products to your precious feathered friends because you are dedicated to giving them the best nutrition possible.

WE THANK YOU FOR TRUSTING US!
Happy Thanksgiving to you and yours
Lafeber Company

Source: Lafeber Company website: http://lafebercares.com/.

Based on a study of virtual communities, the authors show how the feeling of gratitude a community member feels towards another member may also impact commitment and co-shopping. Like anger, gratitude may affect all phases of consumer behaviour, as shown in Table 4.6.

Table 4.6   Anger and gratitude during the various phases of the purchase and consumption process

	Emotions	
	Anger	Gratitude
Phases of the purchase and consumption process	*SELECTED EXAMPLES*	
Perception of need, search for information and assessment of alternatives	Confused merchandising can generate great annoyance for the visitor to a sales outlet who is looking for a particular product	A careful and attentive guidance service (e.g., didactic guidance in choosing a training course) generates gratitude
Moment of purchase	An irritating sales assistant can generate a sense of anger	The dedication of a sales assistant who works hard to find the 'ideal product' for a customer can elicit the purchaser's gratitude
Moment of consumption	A product that works badly due to the inattentiveness of the producer elicits anger	The performance of a service that exceeds expectations can induce gratitude as well as surprise
Phases subsequent to purchase and consumption	The 'aggravating behaviour' of the service provider can trigger a vicious circle of anger	Certain initiatives reserved for customers after they purchase and consume a product can generate gratitude. For example, a phone call from a shopkeeper informing a customer of a promotional sale is gratefully appreciated

NOTE

1. See www.justsell.com, www.mtctraining.com and www.salesvantage.com.

5. Consumption emotions and the determination of post-consumption behaviour

This chapter contains the empirical verifications of the predictive model of post-purchase behaviour illustrated in Chapter 1. In particular, sections 5.1 and 5.2 refer to the psychological and marketing literature that led to the definition of the *frame*, literature that was extensively presented in Chapters 2, 3 and 4. Here I will specifically refer to the combinations of appraisals that originate the different emotions analysed before and the action tendencies that derive from them. Section 5.2 illustrates the investigation method used for the empirical verification of the predictive model while section 5.3 discusses the results obtained and the managerial implications deriving from the study. The proposed investigation was conducted using the traditional 'paper and pen' research methods based on explicit measures. Being aware of the important limitations that characterize this measurement of emotions, this last chapter will end with an overview about the use of implicit methods for measuring consumption emotions.

5.1 EMOTIONS AS DETERMINANTS OF POST-CONSUMPTION BEHAVIOURS: THE DERIVATION OF A PREDICTIVE MODEL

As examined in Chapter 2, marketing scholars have always attempted to determine the predictive factors of post-purchase behaviour, such as repurchase or abandonment, complaining, positive or negative word of mouth, and so on (e.g., Gronhaug and Zaltman, 1977; Day and Ash, 1978; Krishnan and Valle, 1979; Day, 1983; Andreasen, 1985; Singh, 1990; Stephens and Gwinner, 1998; Athnassopoulos et al., 2001; Mittal and Kamakura, 2001; Caruana, 2002; Yi and La,

2004; Gustafsson et al., 2005). In Chapter 2, we highlighted how this behaviour is tendentially considered to be a consequence of satisfaction or dissatisfaction (Yi, 1989; Anderson and Fornell, 1994).

As a matter of fact, as suggested in the subsequent chapters, dissatisfaction is, on the one hand, probably not the only determining factor of unfavourable post-purchase behaviour for the company (Day, 1983). On the other hand, it does not predict *a particular* negative response (Bougie et al., 2003). For example, it is not clear in which situations dissatisfaction leads to a complaint or abandonment, rather than to negative word of mouth (Nyer, 1997).

Satisfaction, in turn, cannot be considered as sufficient for favourable post-purchase behaviour. Moreover, this emotion could also generate negative responses: a consumer, in fact, could be ready to abandon brand A, a brand she is satisfied with, for brand B, which gratifies her even more.

It is not perfectly clear at the moment, therefore, what other variables affect the relationship between satisfaction/dissatisfaction and post-purchase behaviour (Nyer, 1997; Bougie et al., 2003). However, managing to predict the specific responses of consumers is of fundamental importance for marketing people. For example, we can see that some dissatisfied customers prefer to leave the brand or spread their negative opinion rather than ask for compensation directly from the producer or provider of the disappointing service. This is 'invisible' behaviour that is particularly dangerous for the firm (Richins, 1987). This behaviour does allow the firm to 'remedy the situation' and, therefore, to recover the relationship with the customer (Hirschman, 1970; Lapidus and Pinkerton, 1995).

Why do some dissatisfied consumers complain while others vent their frustration through negative word of mouth? This is a crucial question for marketing managers, partly because negative word of mouth can irreparably damage the reputation of the firm, thus preventing it from satisfying an extensive potential target. Fornell and Wernerfelt (1987) go as far as to say that encouraging complaints is an excellent marketing strategy for maintaining customer loyalty. At this stage, the utility of the model we set out to test, a model aiming precisely at predicting *specific* post-purchase behaviour, should be clear.

In Chapter 2, I presented a series of variables affecting the relationship between satisfaction (dissatisfaction) and post-purchase behaviour: the judgement of attribution, the characteristics of the

sector, the perception by customers that their claims have been effectively heard, the behaviour of customers as regards complaining, the
importance attributed to the product and customer satisfaction.

Nyer (1997) developed a predictive model of the various consumer
responses that can potentially include all the above variables that
come into play. More precisely, he demonstrated how some of these
variables can be considered as *appraisals* of specific emotions and
how the latter are able to determine certain types of post-purchase
behaviour. In particular, he verified how consumer expectations, the
importance attributed to the product and the perception that a complaint has been effectively attended to or not determine joy, anger,
sadness and satisfaction. Nyer (ibid.) also demonstrated that these
emotions mediate the relationship between the above appraisals and
the responses of the consumer.

A similar model to Nyer's was proposed by Bougie et al. (2003).
In particular, the authors demonstrated that the antecedents of the
expectations and of the judgement of attribution elicit anger and
dissatisfaction. In turn, these emotions provoke different reactions
in consumers. Also in this case, the authors show how the emotive
variables partially mediate the effects of the cognitive antecedents
mentioned in negative word of mouth, complaint and abandonment.

The studies by Nyer (1997) and Bougie et al. (2003) inspired the
construction of the model presented in this text. The proposed *frame*,
therefore, starts from these researches and sets out to extend them in
two directions: (1) I wish to consider other consumption emotions,
such as the sense of guilt and gratitude – variables, as seen above,
that tend to be neglected in marketing studies; and (2) I intend to
formulate a model capable of predicting additional post-purchase
behaviour, such as repurchasing.

In Chapter 1, with special reference to the cognitive theory, I
highlighted how emotions are not elicited from a specific event but
rather from thought on a particular happening (appraisal). Precisely
with reference to appraisal typologies, the model in question will
not comprise all the possible cognitive antecedents considered by
psychological literature but only those that seem to be particularly
relevant for the studies on consumer behaviour: the *desirability* and
causation of an event, appraisals presented in Chapter 1.

As examined in Chapter 2, desirability is an antecedent of happiness (unhappiness): it is an appraisal close to the concept of confir-
mation/disconfirmation of the expectations indicated in section 2.3,

an antecedent of satisfaction. In fact, satisfaction can be considered a particular declination of the emotion of 'happiness', a variant that features a lower arousal content.

In the light of these considerations, we can suppose that, in the demand analysis and psychological spheres:

Hypothesis 1a: Desirability generates happiness in the consumer.

Hypothesis 1b: Undesirability generates unhappiness in the consumer.

These assumptions have already been widely tested and verified in psychological literature. However, it seems important to retest them as they are important pillars of the model in question.

The appraisal of causation is defined in Chapter 1: as soon as a subject examines an event, she can feel responsible for it or attribute responsibility to third parties or to circumstances. When the event is classified as desirable and it is attributed to circumstances the subject will be happy; when, instead, the event is considered as undesirable, the emotion elicited is unhappiness. Moreover, in Chapter 3 we indicated how causation is an antecedent of a sense of guilt or pride in the particular case in which an individual accepts full responsibility for the consequences. Anger and gratitude, instead, involve the attribution of failure or success to third parties (see Chapter 4). Therefore, in the demand analysis and purely psychological spheres, we can say that:

Hypothesis 2a: The gratitude of a consumer is elicited by a desirable result for which the producer or service provider is responsible.

Hypothesis 2b: The sense of guilt of a consumer is elicited by an undesirable result for which the consumer is responsible.

Hypothesis 2c: The pride of consumer is elicited by a desirable result for which the consumer is responsible.

Hypothesis 2d: The anger of a consumer is elicited by an undesirable result for which the producer or service provider is responsible.

Table 5.1 presents the first two assumptions, illustrating the interaction between the appraisal of desirability and that of causation.

Table 5.1   The first two research assumptions

		Desirability of the event	
		Undesirable event	Desirable event
Causation of	Responsibility	*Scenario 1*	*Scenario 2*
the event	attributed to	Sadness	Happiness
	oneself	Sense of guilt	Pride
	Responsibility	*Scenario 3*	*Scenario 4*
	attributed to	Sadness	Happiness
	the producer	Anger	Gratitude
	or service		
	provider		
	Responsibility	*Scenario 5*	*Scenario 6*
	attributed to	Sadness	Happiness
	circumstances		

The specific combinations of the levels of the two cognitive ante-cedents generate happiness, unhappiness, sense of guilt, anger, pride and gratitude. The experimental stimuli (scenarios) used to reproduce these interactions will be discussed in the next section.

Concerning tendency to action instead, in Chapter 4 we pointed out that anger stimulates antagonism (opposition and attack) and reaction (I want to overcome the obstacle), an aggression aiming to modify the outcome of an event. With specific reference to the consumer, Yi and Baumgartner (2004) show how customers desire to meet the producer, wish to express their disappointment in order to obtain compensation or an apology. The antagonism described by Frijda (1987) is therefore expressed in the purchase and consumption processes through a specific consumer response: complaining. In this sense, Bougie et al. (2003) demonstrate how the emotion of anger mediates the relationship between ignored expectations and complaining.

On the contrary, the authors declare, but do not demonstrate, that the sadness of a consumer does not generate the same response. In Chapter 2, in fact, we saw that sadness is associated with passive tendencies to action, such as renunciation, feeling lost and crying: a consumer who is simply dissatisfied tends not express his or her disappointment. In the light of these considerations, we can assume that:

Hypothesis 3a: In the event of an undesirable result, it is more probable that the anger of a consumer will induce them to complain rather than vent their dissatisfaction.

Hypothesis 3b: In the event of an undesirable result, the greater the anger felt by the consumer, the more likely it is that they will complain.

In the case of a sense of guilt, instead, the most probable tendency to action is accepting one's responsibility (Folkman et al., 1986), that is, the *amendment and commitment* discussed in Chapter 3. Accepting one's responsibilities should lead the consumer to decide not to complain and not to generate negative word of mouth:

Hypothesis 4:   In the event of an undesirable result, the sense of guilt felt by a consumer inhibits both complaint and negative word of mouth.

As indicated in Chapters 2 and 4, psychological literature has neglected to study the tendency to action of passive emotions. These tendencies are indicated fairly vaguely and are very often not specifically illustrated for individual positive emotions (Fredrickson, 2004). Gratitude should promote actions aiming to improve the benefactor's well-being ('I want to take care of'). On the contrary, happiness leads to empty, purposeless activation ('exuberance'). According to Morales (2005), gratitude therefore stimulates one to fully recognize the value of the product that generated this feeling. This book sets out to extend Morales' conclusions, establishing further relationships of cause and effect between gratitude and other types of behaviour that are favourable to the firm. Lastly, we illustrate the opinion of Louro et al. (2005) according to whom pride inhibits post-purchase behaviour that is favourable to the firm, such as repurchasing. Therefore:

Hypothesis 5a: In the event of a desirable result, the gratitude of the consumer, but not their happiness and pride, strengthens their intention to repurchase.

Hypothesis 5b: In the event of a desirable result, the greater the consumer's sense of gratitude, the greater the probability of positive word of mouth and repurchase.

5.2 EMPIRICAL ASSESSMENT OF THE MODEL[1]

In order to test the hypotheses, a two-factor goal congruence/incongruence X agency experiment was performed. Respondents were randomly assigned to one of six conditions (see Table 5.1) and responses to appropriate emotions and action were measured as dependent variables. The method that was used to create experimental manipulations was similar to one suggested by Roseman (1991) where participants read brief stories about consumption experiences of various protagonists. In these stories, information relevant to the appraisals was systematically varied, and subjects rated the intensity of the emotions that they believed the protagonists felt in response to the events, as well their predicted action tendencies. Figure 5.1 presents example scenario 3.

Multi-item scales were reused to measure the target emotions. The specific categories and items (listed in parentheses) used for the respective emotion were as follows: sadness (sorrow, dissatisfaction), happiness (happiness, gladness, satisfaction), guilt (guilt, remorse) and anger (annoyance, dislike). Single items were used to measure

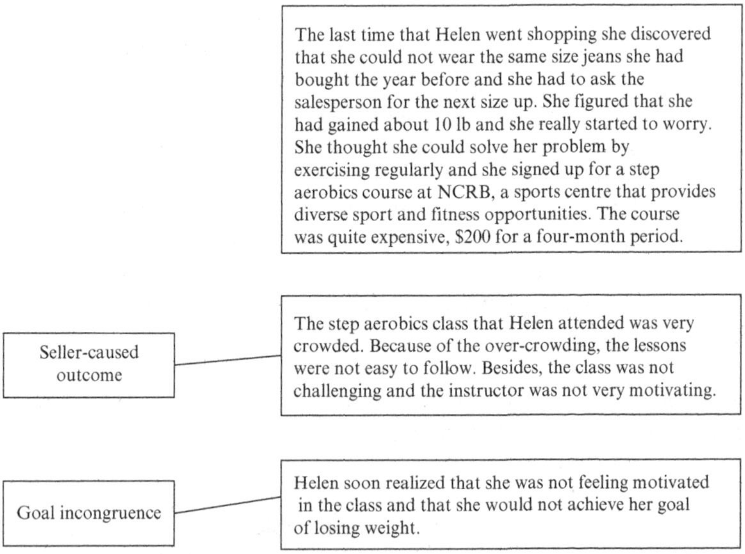

The last time that Helen went shopping she discovered that she could not wear the same size jeans she had bought the year before and she had to ask the salesperson for the next size up. She figured that she had gained about 10 lb and she really started to worry. She thought she could solve her problem by exercising regularly and she signed up for a step aerobics course at NCRB, a sports centre that provides diverse sport and fitness opportunities. The course was quite expensive, $200 for a four-month period.

Seller-caused outcome — The step aerobics class that Helen attended was very crowded. Because of the over-crowding, the lessons were not easy to follow. Besides, the class was not challenging and the instructor was not very motivating.

Goal incongruence — Helen soon realized that she was not feeling motivated in the class and that she would not achieve her goal of losing weight.

Figure 5.1   Scenario 3: seller-caused outcome X goal incongruence

Question 1
How intensely was Helen feeling each of the following emotions at the end of the story?
(Circle your answer in each row)

	Not at all				Moderately						Very intensely
Remorse	0	1	2	3	4	5	6	7	8	9	10
Dissatisfaction	0	1	2	3	4	5	6	7	8	9	10
Gladness	0	1	2	3	4	5	6	7	8	9	10
Dislike	0	1	2	3	4	5	6	7	8	9	10
Satisfaction	0	1	2	3	4	5	6	7	8	9	10
Sorrow	0	1	2	3	4	5	6	7	8	9	10
Guilt	0	1	2	3	4	5	6	7	8	9	10
Annoyance	0	1	2	3	4	5	6	7	8	9	10
Happiness	0	1	2	3	4	5	6	7	8	9	10
Pride	0	1	2	3	4	5	6	7	8	9	10
Gratitude	0	1	2	3	4	5	6	7	8	9	10

Question 2
Now please indicate how likely Helen will perform each of the following (circle your answer in each row)

	Very unlikely	Unlikely	Neither unlikely or likely	Likely	Very likely
Helen will complain to the person at the NCRB fitness office about the class	1	2	3	4	5
Helen will complain to her friends about NCRB	1	2	3	4	5
Helen will recommend NCRB to her friends	1	2	3	4	5
Helen will sign up for new classes at NCRB when she decides to exercise regularly	1	2	3	4	5

Figure 5.2   The questionnaire

gratitude, pride and the four post-consumption behaviours (see Figure 5.2).

The aim of the experiment is to demonstrate that the different combinations of the two appraisals predicted the appropriate emotions (Hypotheses 1 and 2) and that these emotions predict relevant consumption behaviours (Hypotheses 3, 4 and 5).

A total of 192 participants was asked to read one of the different versions of the stories. Then participants answered the questions measuring the dependent variables. All respondents were women because the content of the six scenarios referred to women and the protagonist was a woman in each case. Women were expected to consider the scenarios relevant and adequately involving. Respondents were graduate students at an Italian Business School in Milan. Information was analysed from 182 completed surveys.

Table 5.2   Factor analysis

Measures	Happiness/sadness	Guilt	Anger
Sorrow	−0.81		
Dissatisfaction	−0.82		
Gladness	0.97		
Happiness	0.96		
Satisfaction	0.98		
Remorse		0.88	
Guilt		0.83	
Annoyance			0.74
Dislike			0.79

Results

A maximum likelihood analysis followed by a promax rotation on the measures of the dependent variables measures showed that happiness, sadness, anger and guilt were measured well by the nine emotion items and loaded on the predicted factors (see Table 5.2). Consistent with the psychology literature, happiness and sadness were expected to belong to the same factor and to show a negative correlation with the other items. The output was a three-factor solution. The three-factor solution accounted for 87 per cent of the total variance and each item loaded highly on its hypothesized factor and relatively low on the non-hypothesized factors.

An omnibus test using multivariate analysis of variance (MANOVA) was conducted with happiness, sadness, guilt, anger and gratitude as dependent variables. As hypothesized, while guilt, anger, gratitude and pride were functions of significant two-way interaction, happiness and sadness were produced by main effects as a consequence of goal congruence/incongruence. The specific findings are presented below.

Hypothesis 1
In order to test the first hypothesis, a one-way ANOVA was run with goal congruence/incongruence as a single factor and happiness as the dependent variable. The results revealed a significant effect of goal congruence/incongruence (F (1, 179) = 1413.46, $p<0.001$), which shows higher happiness for goal congruence (M = 8.89) than goal

incongruence (M = 0.70). Also sadness exhibited the presence of a significant goal congruence/incongruence (F (1, 178) = 389.34, p<0.001) effect: the degree of sadness is higher under condition of incongruence (M = 6.72) than under condition of congruence (M = 0.79).

Hypothesis 2
An ANOVA conducted on gratitude confirmed a significant goal congruence/incongruence X agency interaction: F (2, 176) = 20.84, p<0.001. A planned contrast showed that gratitude experienced in the case of the goal congruent seller-outcome (M = 6.67) was higher than the average gratitude experienced in the other cases (M = 1.21): t (180) = −10.73, p<0.0011.

Also, the ANOVA conducted on guilt confirmed the presence of a significant goal congruence/incongruence X agency interaction: F (2, 175) = 26.72, p<0.001. Furthermore, a planned contrast revealed that guilt experienced in the case of incongruent self-caused outcome (M = 8.10) was higher than the average guilt felt in the other scenarios (M = 1.93), t (179) = −11.64, p<0.0012.

Moreover, an ANOVA was run with goal congruence/incongruence and agency as factors and pride as the dependent variable. The interaction significantly predicted pride (F (2, 176) = 37.00, p<0.001). Pride felt in the case of the congruent self-outcome is significantly higher than the average pride felt in the other cases, M = 9.48 vs M = 2.71, t (180) = −9.5, p<0.0013.

Finally, an ANOVA was run with goal congruence/incongruence and agency as factors and anger as the dependent variable. The interaction significantly predicted anger (F (2, 174) = 4.04, p<0.05). Moreover, anger felt in the case of the incongruent seller-outcome is significantly higher than the average anger felt in the other cases, M = 3.88 vs M = 2.17, and t (178) = −3.96, p<0.0014.

Hypotheses 3 and 4
To investigate Hypotheses 3 and 4, the correlations between the six emotions and the two negative post-consumption behaviours were analysed: complaining and negative word of mouth. These correlations are shown in Table 5.3.

As forecast, the findings show a positive correlation between anger and complaining (r = 0.18, p<0.05), while the correlation between sadness and complaining was not significant. Also as predicted, two significant negative correlations between guilt and the two negative

Table 5.3   Correlations between emotions and complaining and negative word of mouth

R	Complaint	Negative word of mouth
Happiness	n.s.	n.s.
Sadness	n.s.	0.17*
Anger	0.18*	0.25**
Guilt	−0.52**	−0.41**
Gratitude	n.s.	n.s.
Pride	n.s.	n.s.

Note: * Significant at $\alpha = 0.05$; ** significant at $\alpha = 0.01$.

Table 5.4   Regression of complaint and negative word of mouth on emotions

	Complaint	Negative word of mouth
Independent variable		
Happiness β	n.s.	n.s.
Sadness β	n.s.	0.33**
Anger β	n.s.	n.s.
Guilt β	−0.60**	−0.54**
Gratitude β	n.s.	n.s.
Pride β	n.s.	n.s.
Significance of F	0.00	0.00
R^2	0.35	0.32
Adjusted R^2	0.31	0.27

Note: * Significant at $\alpha = 0.05$; ** significant at $\alpha = 0.01$.

post-consumption behaviours were found ($r = -0.52$ and $r = -0.41$, respectively, $p<0.01$).

To verify the causal relations between emotions and the two negative action tendencies, two multiple regression analyses were performed under condition of goal incongruence. Table 5.4 summarizes the results of the regressions. The analyses show that, when goal incongruence occurred, neither anger nor sadness predicted complaining. Finally, guilt inhibited both complaining behaviour ($\beta = -0.60$, $p<0.01$) and negative word of mouth ($\beta = -0.54$, $p<0.01$) as hypothesized.

Table 5.5   Correlations between emotions and repurchase intention and positive word of mouth

R	Repurchase intention	Positive word of mouth
Happiness	0.22*	0.28**
Sadness	−0.22*	−0.21*
Anger	−0.25*	−0.31**
Guilt	n.s.	n.s.
Gratitude	0.66**	0.78**
Pride	0.22*	0.31**

Note: * Significant at $\alpha = 0.05$; ** significant at $\alpha = 0.01$.

Hypothesis 5

To study the relations between emotions and the two positive post-consumption behaviours, the correlations between these variables were analysed (see Table 5.5). As predicted, the correlation between gratitude and repurchase intention is higher than between happiness and the same behaviour ($r = 0.66$, $p<0.01$ vs $r = 0.22$, $p<0.05$). Moreover, it is higher than the one between pride and repurchase intention ($r = 0.66$, $p<0.01$ vs $r = 0.22$, $p<0.05$).The findings also show a higher correlation between gratitude and positive word of mouth than happiness and positive word of mouth ($r = 0.78$, $p<0.01$ vs $r = 0.28$, $p<0.01$). Besides, the correlation between gratitude and positive word of mouth is higher than the one between pride and the positive word of mouth ($r = 0.78$, $p<0.01$ vs $r = 0.31$, $p<0.01$).

Further, to analyse the relationships between the emotions and the two positive behaviours, two multiple regression analyses were run under condition of goal congruence (see Table 5.6). The findings support both hypotheses: gratitude determines repurchase intentions and positive word of mouth, while intentions and positive word of mouth were not influenced by happiness and pride, as hypothesized.

The previous analyses demonstrate that cognitive appraisals of agency and goal congruence/incongruence determine consumption emotions and that these emotions predict particular behaviours. Next, it is important to test whether emotions mediate the relations between cognitive appraisals and behaviours. To investigate these effects a step-down analysis using MANOVA was performed

Table 5.6   Regression of repurchase intention and positive word of mouth on emotions

	Repurchase intention	Positive word of mouth
Independent variable		
Happiness β	n.s.	n.s.
Sadness β	n.s.	n.s.
Anger β	n.s.	n.s.
Guilt β	n.s.	n.s.
Gratitude β	0.70**	0.79**
Pride β	n.s.	n.s.
Significance of F	0.00	0.00
R^2	0.52	0.71
Adjusted R^2	0.48	0.69

Note: * Significant at $\alpha = 0.05$; ** significant at $\alpha = 0.01$.

(Bagozzi and Yi, 1989). The first test of this analysis is designed to show whether the predicted combination of appraisals have significant effects on emotions and post-consumption behaviours. Once these effects are verified, the second step is to demonstrate that the effects that appraisals have on behaviours are due to the mediating role of emotions. Table 5.7 summarizes the result of the step-down MANOVA.

The first test is a MANOVA in which the two appraisals and their combination are the independent variables and each emotion (gratitude and guilt) and the behaviours (positive word of mouth, negative word of mouth, complaint and repurchase) are the dependent variables. The multivariate effects were significant: the predicted combination of appraisals significantly determine the dependent variables. Under the second test, the dependent variables are the behaviours and the two emotions are covaried out. A significant effect of the predicted combination of appraisals on the behaviours was obtained. That is, once the effects of the emotions have been partialled out, the predicted combination of appraisals affects the behaviours. Thus the analysis shows that emotions do not totally mediate the relationship between appraisals and behaviours. In other words, emotions partially mediate the effects of appraisals on behaviour.

Table 5.7   Step-down analysis (p values of the multivariate F-test statistic)

(a)

Effect	Step 1 Dependent variables: gratitude, repurchase intention and positive word of mouth (covariates: none)	Step 2 Dependent variables: repurchase intention and positive word of mouth (covariates: gratitude)
Goal congruence/ incongruence	0.00	0.01
Agency	0.00	0.90
Goal congruence/ incongruence X agency	0.00	0.00

(b)

Effect	Step 1 Dependent variables: guilt, complaining and negative word of mouth (covariates: none)	Step 2 Dependent variables: complaining and negative word of mouth (covariates: guilt)
Goal congruence/ incongruence	0.00	0.00
Agency	0.00	0.00
Goal congruence/ incongruence X agency	0.00	0.00

5.3   DISCUSSION

Post-purchase phenomena are of special interest to managers because such behaviours determine the success or the failure of the business. Because these behaviours are not directly controllable, knowledge about antecedents that can indirectly influence these behaviours is extremely valuable. Ideally, these antecedents should be managerially controllable, for example via advertising copy or sales representative presentations. The objective is to influence emotions and decisions through these controllable stimuli so as to change behaviour.

Under Hypothesis 1, 'goal congruence/incongruence' elicits the negative emotion, sadness, and the positive emotion, happiness. Nevertheless, these emotions by themselves do not predict the different post-consumption behaviour outcomes. By contrast, under Hypothesis 2, the findings show that the interaction between goal congruence/incongruence and agency appraisals elicits two key emotions: gratitude and guilt, which have important roles in predicting different behaviours. In particular, gratitude leads to positive word of mouth and repurchase intentions. Guilt, where consumers accept their responsibility for prior actions and the negative outcome, inhibits negative word of mouth and complaining behaviours.

The predicted attributions of other-directed anger did not influence behaviour outcomes. This result was probably due to the choice that was made in the type of service for the experiment. In fact, as sports enthusiasts know very well, it is very difficult to get physically fit when one is less than diligent in exercising: thus, a sense of self-anger sometimes follows bad fitness results (for research on self-anger, see Ben-Ze'ev, 2000). In future research, the two forms of anger (self vs other directed) should be distinguished more clearly, especially with reference to their different effects on post-consumption behaviours.

The findings show that particular combinations of antecedents determine specific emotions, that these emotions predict different post-consumption behaviours, and that these emotions partially mediate the effects of the manipulated appraisals on post-consumptions behaviours. More precisely, the results of this study suggest that attributions influence how consumers feel in different cases of positive and negative outcomes, and these emotions imply different consumer behavioural responses to service success or failure.

5.4   USE OF NEUROSCIENTIFIC METHODS TO STUDY AND MEASURE EMOTIONS[2]

Classic survey-based academic research such as the work presented in the sections above are vulnerable to various types of error: non-response error due to refusals, inaccuracy in responses and errors caused by interviewers (Aaker et al., 2007). With regard to emotions, studies based on explicit measures involve the risk of inaccurate responses. Specifically, the potential unwillingness to respond accurately (i.e., deliberate falsification) as well as unconscious misrepresentations (i.e., the unconscious provision of inaccurate answers) may compromise the reliability of the study (Arbore et al., 2012).

Distinguishing between implicit and explicit measures has been a major subject of debate in psychology literature. Explicit measures operate in a conscious mode and are exemplified by traditional self-reported measures such as the questionnaire shown in Figure 5.2. On the other hand, implicit measures are assumed to operate in an unconscious mode, reflecting an automatic mental process that is beyond the individual's control and awareness (Wilson et al., 2000). Explicit measures are an important component of any consumption research programme, but they may provide only a partial picture of the consumer's underlying cognitions. In fact, as discussed in the first chapter of the book, the stimuli that elicit emotions may also be unconscious, and consumers may not be completely aware of the emotions they experience. Moreover, only some of the action tendencies elicited by emotions are detectable by an external observer (i.e., blushing as a consequence of embarrassment). Other effects, such as the secretion of endorphins and its impact on neural pathways, cannot be detected by traditional research tools. In all of these cases, the measurement issue is better addressed with the help of implicit measures such as the ones introduced in this section. Despite increased attention to non-conscious processes and implicit measures in academic psychology, business and market research have devoted only little energy to this stream of literature (Cohen and Chakravarti, 1990; Simonson et al., 2001).

With regard to emotions and the neurosciences, scholars began to analyse affective states using instruments that allow a representation of the brain's metabolic activities during the 1990s. One of the most important contributions of neuroscience to emotional studies is its ability to localize emotions: different emotions activate different areas of the brain, and thus temporary changes in different areas suggest that the consumer is experiencing a specific emotion.

New methods of brain scanning have become increasingly powerful and effective in detecting emotions based on their location in different areas of the brain. Functional magnetic resonance imaging (fMRI), electroencephalography (EEG), magnetoencephalography

(MEG) and brain positron emission tomography (PET) offer promising means of investigating and better understanding of consumption emotions.

For example, Knutson and Greer (2008) used fMRI to show how pleasure activates the nucleus accumbens (the neural system where fear and pleasure are processed) when a sample of males was exposed to erotic images. At the other end of the spectrum, the insular cortex processes negative emotions such as displeasure or disgust. Thus, typical emotions in the consumer experience may start in either of the two areas: the former when we enjoy a restaurant with three Michelin stars, the latter when we think about the bill we will pay afterwards.

Thanks to PET, Cahill and McGaugh (1998) demonstrated the role played by the amygdala in preserving memories of emotions. The scholars asked a sample of subjects to watch one emotionally upsetting movie and then a second, milder one. After three weeks, the subjects underwent a memory test that demonstrated that they were able to recall the emotionally disturbing movie better. PET pinpointed higher metabolic activity in the right amygdala during the screening of the upsetting movie. The results support the hypothesis that the amygdala is the brain area responsible for emotional learning and storage.

The anticipated emotions presented in the first chapter may also be detected using brain scanning techniques. Combining PET and fMRI, Hamann et al. (2004) demonstrated that the pleasure that consumers anticipate when they are about to listen to a piece of music may be detected by the secretion of dopamine. Moreover, another study by Salimpoor et al. (2011) on music consumption revealed that two different neural pathways are activated by anticipated emotions and consumption emotions. Before a subject listens to music, neural activity in the caudate nuclei prevails, while activity in the nucleus accumbens predominates in the case of previously experienced emotions.

Unfortunately, the experimental setting that characterizes all these studies makes it rather difficult to recreate the complexity of the consumer's 'natural habitat' (e.g., the monitoring of brain activity during a real-world shopping experience). However, initial steps have already been taken in order to fill this gap. For example, research conducted by 1to1lab for Procter and Gamble (Stingo and Gallucci, 2007) employed EEG in order to study the emotions, such as anxiety and pleasure, felt by consumers during a shopping expedition in the 'natural habitat' of a supermarket. Therefore, future and more ambitious studies could enhance the external validity of these research designs by conducting neuroscientific marketing experiments in the field.

NOTES

1. The original source of publication of the empirical assessment of the presented model is Soscia (2007). Paragraphs 5.2 and 5.3 are reproduced with permission of John Wiley & Sons Inc.
2. This section was written by Francesco Gallucci.

References

Aaker, J.L. and A.Y. Lee (2001), '"I" seek pleasures and "we" avoid pains: the role of self-regulatory goals in information processing and persuasion', *Journal of Consumer Research*, **28** (1), 33–49.

Aaker, David A., V. Kumar and George, S. Day (eds) (2007), *Marketing Research*, New York: John Wiley & Sons.

Addis, Michela and Isabella Soscia (2006), 'Acquisti, consumo ed emozioni', in *Management*, Volume 11, Milano: Università Bocconi Editore.

Agrawal, N. and A. Duhachek (2010), 'Emotional compatibility and the effectiveness of antidrinking messages: a defensive processing perspective on shame and guilt', *Journal of Marketing Research*, **47** (2), 263–73.

Anderson, E.W. and C. Fornell (1994), 'A customer satisfaction research prospectus', in L.T. Rust and L.R. Oliver (eds), *Service Quality. New Directions in Theory and Practice*, Thousand Oaks, CA: Sage Publications, pp. 241–69.

Andreasen, A.R. (1985), 'Consumer responses to dissatisfaction in loose monopolies', *Journal of Consumer Research*, **12** (2), 135–41.

Arbore, A., I. Soscia and G. Miniero (2012), 'Avoiding social desirability bias: computer-based lie detection techniques', unpublished working paper, Università Bocconi.

Athnassopoulos, A., S. Gounaris and V. Stathakopoulos (2001), 'Behavioural responses to customer satisfaction: an empirical study', *European Journal of Marketing*, **35** (5/6), 687–707.

Averill, James R. (1982), *Anger and Aggression: An Essay on Emotion*, New York: Springer.

Babakus, E., P. Tat and W. Cunningham (1988), 'Coupon redemption: a motivational perspective', *Journal of Consumer Marketing*, **5** (2), 37–43.

Bagozzi, R.P. (1999), 'Happiness', in David Levinson, James J. Ponzetti and Peter F. Jorgensen (eds), *Encyclopedia of Human Emotions*, New York: Macmillan, pp. 317–24.

Bagozzi, R.P. and D.J. Moore (1994), 'Public service advertisements: emotions and empathy guide prosocial behavior', *Journal of Marketing*, **58** (1), 56–70.

Bagozzi, R.P. and Y. Yi (1989), 'On the use of structural equation models in experimental design', *Journal of Marketing Research*, **26** (3), 271–84.

Bagozzi, R.P., H. Baumgartner and R. Pieters (1998), 'Goal-directed emotions', *Cognition and Emotion*, **12** (1), 1–26.

Bagozzi, R.P., M. Gopinath and P.U. Nyer (1999), 'The role of emotions in marketing', *Journal of Academy of Marketing Science*, **27** (2), 184–206.

Bagozzi, Richard P., Zeynep Gurhan-Canli and Joseph R. Priester (2002), *The Social Psychology of Consumer Behaviour*, Buckingham: Open University Press.

Basil, D.Z., N.M. Ridgway and M.D. Basil (2006), 'Guilt appeals: the mediating effect of responsibility', *Psychology & Marketing*, **23** (12), 1035–54.

Batra, R. and O.T. Athola (1990), 'Measuring the hedonic and utilitarian sources of consumer attitudes', *Marketing Letters*, **2** (2), 159–70.

Batra, R., A. Ahuvia and R.P. Bagozzi (2012), 'Brand love', *Journal of Marketing*, **76** (2), 1–16.

Baumeister, R.F. (2002), 'Yielding to temptation: self-control failure, impulsive purchasing and consumer behavior', *Journal of Consumer Research*, **28** (4), 670–76.

Baumeister, R.F., A.M. Stillwell and T.F. Heatherton (1994), 'Guilt: an interpersonal approach', *Psychological Bulletin*, **115** (2), 243–67.

Bennett, R. (1998), 'Shame, guilt & responses to non-profit & public sector ads', *International Journal of Advertising*, **17** (4), 483–99.

Ben-Ze'ev, A. (2000), *The Subtlety of Emotions*, Cambridge, MA: MIT Press.

Beverland, M.B., S.M. Kates, A. Lindgreen and E. Chung (2010), 'Exploring consumer conflict management in service encounters', *Journal of the Academy of Marketing Science*, **38** (5), 617–33.

Blodgett, J.G., K.L. Wakefield and J.H. Barnes (1995), 'The effects of customer service on consumer complaining behavior', *Journal of Services Marketing*, **9** (4), 31–42.

Bonifield, C. and C. Cole (2007), 'Affective response to service failure: anger, regret, and retaliatory versus conciliatory responses', *Marketing Letters*, **18** (1), 85–99.

Bougie, R., R. Pieters and M. Zeelenberg (2003), 'Angry customers don't come back, they get back: the experience and behavioral implications of anger and dissatisfaction in services', *Journal of Academy of Marketing Science*, **31** (4), 377–93.

Boyd, H.C. (1995), 'Effects of fear appeal format and consumer personality on ad processing and persuasion: a preliminary analysis', *Marketing Letters*, **6** (3), 211–20.

Bozinoff, L. and M. Ghingold (1983), 'Evaluating guilt arousing marketing communications', *Journal of Business Research*, **11** (2), 243–55.

Burnett, M.S. and D.A. Lunsford (1994), 'Conceptualizing guilt in the consumer decision-making process', *Journal of Consumer Marketing*, **11** (3), 33–43.

Burroughs, J. and A. Rindfleisch (1997), 'Materialism as a coping mechanism: an inquiry into family disruption', *Advances in Consumer Research*, **24** (1), 89–97.

Cadotte, E.R., R.B. Woodruff and R.L. Jenkins (1987), 'Expectations and norms in models of consumer satisfaction', *Journal of Marketing Research*, **24** (3), 305–14.

Cahill, L. and J.L. McGaugh (1998), 'Mechanisms of emotional arousal and lasting declarative memory', *Trends in Neurosciences*, **21** (7), 294–9.

Canary, Daniel J. and B.A. Semic (1999), 'Anger', in David Levinson, James J. Ponzetti and Peter F. Jorgensen (eds), *Encyclopedia of Human Emotions*, New York: Macmillan, pp. 42–50.

Caruana, A. (2002), 'Service loyalty: the effects of service quality and the mediating role of customer satisfaction', *European Journal of Marketing*, **36** (7/8), 811–29.

Carver, C.S., M.F. Scheier and K. Weintraub (1989), 'Assessing coping strategies: a theoretically based approach', *Journal of Personality and Social Psychology*, **56** (2), 267–83.

Celsi, R.L., L.R. Randall and T.W. Leigh (1993), 'An exploration of high-risk leisure consumption through skydiving', *Journal of Consumer Research*, **20** (1), 1–23.

Chan, K.W. and S.Y. Li (2010), 'Understanding consumer-to-consumer interactions in virtual communities: the salience of reciprocity', *Journal of Business Research*, **63** (9–10), 1033–40.

Chang, C. (2008), 'To donate or not to donate? Product characteristics and framing effects of cause-related marketing on consumer purchase behavior', *Psychology & Marketing*, **25** (12), 1089–110.

Chun, H., V.M. Patrick and D.J. MacInnis (2007), 'Making prudent vs. impulsive choices: the role of anticipated shame and guilt on consumer self-control', *Advances in Consumer Research*, **34**, 715–19.

Clore, G.L., A. Ortony, B. Dienes and F. Fujita (1993), 'Where does anger dwell?', in Robert S. Wyer Jr and Thomas K. Srull (eds), *Perspectives on Anger and Emotion. Advances in Social Cognition*, Hillsdale, NJ: Lawrence Erlbaum, pp. 57–87.

Cochrane, L. and P. Quester (2005), 'Fear in advertising: the influence of consumers' product involvement and culture', *Journal of International Consumer Marketing*, **17** (2/3), 7–27.

Cohen, J.B. and D. Chakravarti (1990), 'Consumer psychology', *Annual Review of Psychology*, **41**, 243–88.

Cotte, J., R.H. Coulter and M.L. Moore (2005), 'Enhancing or disrupting guilt: the role of credibility and perceived manipulative intent', *Journal of Business Research*, **58** (3), 361–8.

Coulter, R.H. and M.B. Pinto (1995), 'Guilt appeals in advertising: what are their effects?', *Journal of Applied Psychology*, **80** (6), 697–705.

Csikszentmihalyi, Mihali (1990), *Flow: The Psychology of Optimal Experience*, New York: Harper Perennial.

Dahl, D.W., H. Honea and R.V. Manchanda (2003), 'The nature of self-reported guilt in consumption contexts', *Marketing Letters*, **14** (3), 159–71.

Dahl, D.W., R.V Manchanda and J.J. Argo (2001), 'Embarrassment in consumer purchase: the role of social presence and purchase familiarity', *Journal of Consumer Research*, **28** (3), 473–81.

Dallimore, K.S., B.A. Sparks and K. Butcher (2007), 'The influence of angry customer outbursts on service providers' facial displays and affective states', *Journal of Service Research*, **10** (1), 78–92.

Day, R.L. (1983), 'Modelling choices among alternative responses to dissatisfaction', *Advances in Consumer Research*, **10** (1), 496–9.

Day, R.L. and S.B. Ash (1978), 'Consumer responses to dissatisfaction with durable products', *Advances in Consumer Research*, **5** (1), 438–44.

Dawson, S. (1988), 'Four motivations for charitable giving: implications for marketing strategy to attract monetary donations for medical research', *Journal of Health Care Marketing*, **8** (2), 31–7.

De Hooge, I.E., S.M. Breugelmans and M. Zeelenberg (2008),

'Not so ugly after all: when shame acts as a commitment device', *Journal of Personality and Social Psychology*, **95** (4), 933–43.

Derbaix, C. and M.T. Pham (1991), 'Affective reactions to consumption situations: a pilot investigation', *Journal of Economic Psychology*, **12** (2), 325–56.

Dolnicar, S. (2005), 'Understanding barriers to leisure travel: tourist fears as a marketing basis', *Journal of Vacation Marketing*, **11** (3), 197–208.

Donovan, R.J. and R. Rossiter (1982), 'Store atmosphere: an environmental psychology approach', *Journal of Retailing*, **58** (1), 34–57.

Duke, C.R., G.M. Pickett, L. Carlson and S.J. Grove (1993), 'A method for evaluating the ethics of fear appeals', *Journal of Public Policy & Marketing*, **12** (1), 120–29.

Eisenberg, N. and R.A. Fabes (1990), 'Empathy: conceptualization, measurement, and relation to prosocial behavior', *Motivation and Emotion*, **14** (2), 131–49.

Elster, Jon (1999), *Strong Feelings. Emotion, Addiction and Human Behavior*, Cambridge, MA: MIT Press.

Engel, James. F. and Roger D. Blackwell (1982), *Consumer Behavior*, New York: Holt, Rinehart, and Wiston.

Erevelles, S. (1998), 'The role of affect in marketing', *Journal of Business Research*, **42** (3), 199–215.

Ferguson, T.J. (1999), 'Guilt emotions', in David Levinson, James J. Ponzetti and Peter F. Jorgensen (eds), *Encyclopedia of Human Emotions*, New York: Macmillan, pp. 307–15.

Folkes, V.S. (1984), 'Consumer reactions to product failure: an attributional approach', *Journal of Consumer Research*, **10** (4), 398–409.

Folkman, S., R.S. Lazarus, C. Dunkel-Schetter, A. DeLongis and R.J. Gruen (1986), 'Dynamics of a stressful encounter: cognitive appraisal, coping, and encounter outcomes', *Journal of Personality and Social Psychology*, **50** (5), 992–1003.

Fornell, C. and B. Wernerfelt (1987), 'Defensive marketing strategy by customer complaint management: a theoretical analysis', *Journal of Marketing Research*, **24** (4), 337–46.

Fredrickson, B.L. (2004), 'Gratitude, like other positive emotions, broadens and builds', in Robert Emmons and Mike E. McCullough (eds), *The Psychology of Gratitude*, New York: Oxford University Press, pp. 145–66.

Frijda, N.H. (1986), *The Emotions*, Cambridge, UK: Cambridge University Press.

Frijda, N.H. (1987), 'Emotion, cognitive structures and action tendency', *Cognition and Emotion*, **1** (2), 115–43.

Frijda, N.H. (1993), 'A place of appraisal in emotion', *Cognition and Emotion*, **7** (314), 357–87.

Frijda, N.H., P. Kuipers and E. Schure (1989), 'Relations among emotion, appraisal, and emotional action readiness', *Journal of Personality and Social Psychology*, **57** (2), 212–28.

Funches, V. (2011), 'The consumer anger phenomena: causes and consequences', *Journal of Service Marketing*, **25** (6), 420–28.

Garbarino, E.C. and J.A. Edell (1997), 'Cognitive effort, affect, and choice', *Journal of Consumer Research*, **24** (2), 147–58.

Gelb, B. and M. Johnson (1995), 'Word-of-mouth communication: causes and consequences', *Journal of Health Care Marketing*, **15** (3), 54–62.

Gelbrich, K. (2010), 'Anger, frustration, and helplessness after service failure: coping strategies and effective information support', *Journal of the Academy of Marketing Science*, **38** (5), 567–85.

Gladden, J.M. and D.C. Funk (2002), 'Developing an understanding of brand associations in team sport: empirical evidence from consumers of professional sport', *Journal of Sport Management*, **16** (1), 54–81.

Goldberg, M.E. and G.J. Gorn (1987), 'Happy and sad TV programs: how they affect reactions to commercials', *Journal of Consumer Research*, **14** (3), 387–403.

Green, E.C. and K. Witte (2006), 'Can fear arousal in public health campaigns contribute to the decline of HIV prevalence?', *Journal of Health Communication*, **11** (3), 245–59.

Gronhaug, K. and G. Zaltman (1977), 'Complainers and non complainers revisited: another look at the data', *Advances in Consumer Research*, **8** (1), 83–7.

Gustafsson, A., M.D. Johnson and I. Roos (2005), 'The effects of customer satisfaction, relationship on commitment dimensions, and triggers on customer retention', *Journal of Marketing*, **69** (4), 210–18.

Halperin, D.T. (2006), 'The controversy over fear arousal in AIDS prevention and lessons from Uganda', *Journal of Health Communication*, **11** (3), 266–7.

Hamann, S., R.A. Herman, C.L. Nolan and K. Wallen (2004), 'Men and women differ in amygdala response to visual sexual stimuli', *Nature Neuroscience*, **7** (4), 411–16.

Hastings, G., M. Stead and J. Webb (2004), 'Fear appeals in social marketing: strategic and ethical reasons for concern', *Psychology & Marketing*, **21** (11), 961–86.

Helson, Henry (1959), 'Adaptation level theory', in Sigmund Koch (ed.), *Psychology: A Study of a Science*, New York: McGraw-Hill, pp. 565–621.

Hesapçı-Sanaktekin, O. (2007), 'Moderating role of valence sequence in mixed affective appeals', *European Advances in Consumer Research*, **8**, 11–14.

Hibbert, S., A. Smith, A. Davies and F. Ireland (2007), 'Guilt appeals: persuasions knowledge and charitable giving', *Psychology & Marketing*, **24** (8), 723–42.

Higgins, E.T. (2002), 'How self-regulation creates distinct values: the case of promotion-prevention decision making', *Journal of Consumer Psychology*, **12** (3), 177–91.

Hirschman, E.C. and M.B. Holbrook (1982), 'Hedonic consumption: emerging concepts, methods and propositions', *Journal of Marketing*, **46** (3), 92–101.

Hirschman, E.C. and B.B. Stern (1999), 'The roles of emotion in consumer research', *Advances in Consumer Research*, **26** (1), 4–11.

Hirschman, Albert O. (1970), *Exit, Voice and Loyalty*, Cambridge, MA: Harvard University Press.

Holbrook, M.B. (1978), 'Beyond attitude structure: toward the informational determinants of attitude', *Journal of Marketing Research*, **15** (4), 545–56.

Holbrook, M.B. and R.M. Schindler (2003), 'Nostalgic bonding: exploring the role of nostalgia in the consumption experience', *Journal of Consumer Behaviour*, **3** (2), 107–27.

Hosany, S. and G. Prayag (2011), 'Patterns of tourists' emotional responses, satisfaction, and intention to recommend', *Journal of Business Research*, doi:10.1016.

Howard, D.J. and C. Gengler (2001), 'Emotional contagion effects on product attitudes', *Journal of Consumer Research*, **28** (2), 189–201.

Howard, John A. and Jagdi N. Sheth (1969), *The Theory of Buyer Behavior*, New York: John Wiley and Sons.

Hsu, M. (2006), 'What matters and changes in condom use? Public perceptions and practices before and after the 2004 HIV/AIDS campaign in Taiwan', *Asian Journal of Communication*, **16** (3), 273–92.

Huhmann, B.A. and T.P. Brotherton (1997), 'A content analysis of guilt appeals in popular magazine advertisements', *Journal of Advertising*, **26** (2), 35–45.

Isen, A.M., T.E. Shalker, M. Clark and L. Karp (1978), 'Positive affect, accessibility of material in memory and behavior: a cognitive loop?', *Journal of Personality and Social Psychology*, **36** (1), 1–12.

Izard, C.E. (1977), *Human Emotions*, New York: Plenum.

Izard, C.E. (1991), *The Psychology of Emotions*, New York: Plenum Press.

Izard, C.E. (1993), 'Four systems of emotion activation: cognitive and noncognitive processes', *Psychological Review*, **100** (1), 68–90.

Jiménez, M. and K.C.C. Yang (2008), 'How guilt level affects green advertising effectiveness?', *Journal of Creative Communication*, **3** (3), 231–54.

Johnson, A.R., M. Matear and M. Thomson (2011), 'A coal in the heart: self-relevance as a post-exit predictor of consumer anti-brand actions', *Journal of Consumer Research*, **38** (1), 108–24.

Keller, P.A., I.M. Lipkus and B.K. Rimer (2002), 'Depressive realism and health risk accuracy: the negative consequences of positive mood', *Journal of Consumer Research*, **29** (1), 57–69.

Keng, K.A., D. Richmond and S. Han (1995), 'Determinants of consumer complaint behavior: a study of Singapore consumers', *Journal of International Consumer Marketing*, **8** (2), 59–68.

Kirby, D. (2006), 'Can fear arousal in public health campaigns contribute to the decline of HIV prevalence?', *Journal of Health Communication*, **11** (3), 262–6.

Kivetz, R. and I. Simonson (2002), 'Earning the right to indulge: effort as a determinant of customer preferences toward frequency program rewards', *Journal of Marketing Research*, **39** (2), 155–70.

Knutson, B. and S.M. Greer (2008), 'Anticipatory affect: neural correlates and consequences for choice', *Philosophical Transactions of Royal Society of London* Series B, **363** (1511), 3771–86.

Krishnan, S. and V.A. Valle (1979), 'Dissatisfaction attributions and consumer complaint behavior', *Advances in Consumer Research*, **6** (1), 445–9.

Kugler, K. and W.H. Jones (1992), 'On conceptualizing and assessing guilt', *Journal of Personality and Social Psychology*, **62** (2), 318–27.

Lapidus, R.S. and L. Pinkerton (1995), 'Customer complaint situations: an equity theory perspective', *Psychology & Marketing*, **12** (2), 105–22.

LaTour, M.S. and R.E. Pitts (1989), 'Using fear appeals in advertising for AIDS prevention in the college-age population', *Journal of Health Care Marketing*, **9** (3), 5–14.

LaTour, M.S. and S.A. Zahra (1988), 'Fear appeals as advertising strategy: should they be used?', *The Journal of Service Marketing*, **2** (4), 5–14.

Lau-Gesk, L. and A. Drolet (2008), 'The publicity self consciousness consumer: prepared to be embarrassed', *Journal of Consumer Psychology*, **18** (2), 127–36.

Lazarus, R.S. (1982), 'Thoughts on the relations between emotion and cognition', *American Psychologist*, **37** (9), 1019–24.

Lazarus, R.S. (1991), *Emotions and Adaptation*, New York: Oxford University Press.

Lazarus, R.S. (1999), *Stress and Emotion*, New York: Springer.

Lee, A.Y. and B. Sternthal (1999), 'The effects of positive mood on memory', *Journal of Consumer Research*, **26** (2), 115–27.

Lee-Wingate, S.N. and K.P. Corfman (2010), 'A little something for me and maybe for you, too: promotions that relieve guilt', *Marketing Letters*, **21** (4), 385–95.

Louro, M.J., R. Pieters and M. Zeelenberg (2005), 'Negative returns on positive emotions: the influence of pride and self-regulatory goals on repurchase decisions', *Journal of Consumer Research*, **31** (4), 833–40.

Luce, M.F. (1998), 'Choosing to avoid: coping with negatively emotion-laden consumer decision', *Journal of Consumer Research*, **24** (4), 409–33.

Lyubomirsky, S., L. King and E. Diener (2005), 'The benefits of frequent positive affect: does happiness lead to success?', *Psychological Bulletin*, **131** (6), 803–55.

MacInnis, D.J. and G. de Mello (2005), 'The concept of hope and its relevance to product evaluation and choice', *Journal of Marketing*, **69** (1), 1–14.

Mano, H. and R.L. Oliver (1993), 'Assessing the dimensionality and the structure of the consumption experience: evaluation, feeling and satisfaction', *Journal of Consumer Research*, **20** (3), 451–66.

Mascolo, Michael F. and Kurt W. Fisher (1995), 'Developmental transformations in appraisals for pride, shame and guilt', in June P. Tangney and Kurt W. Fisher (eds), *Self-conscious Emotions: The Psychology of Shame, Guilt, Embarrassment, and Pride*, New York: Guilford, pp. 64–113.

Mascolo, Michael F., Kurt W. Fisher and Jin Li (2003), 'Dynamic development of component systems of emotions: pride, shame, and guilt in China and the United States', in Richard J. Davidson, Klaus R. Scherer and H. Hill Goldsmith (eds), *Handbook of Affective Sciences*, Oxford: Oxford University Press, pp. 375–408.

Massi Lindsey, L.L. (2005), 'Anticipated guilt as behavioural motivation. An examination of appeals to help unknown others through bone marrow donation', *Human Communication Research*, **31** (4), 453–81.

Mattila, A.S. and J. Wirtz (2004), 'Consumer complaining to firms: the determinants of channel choice', *Journal of Services Marketing*, **18** (2), 147–55.

McCullogh, M.E., J. Tsang and R.A. Emmons (2004), 'Gratitude in intermediate affective terrain: links of grateful moods to individual differences and daily emotional experience', *Journal of Personality and Social Psychology*, **86** (2), 295–309.

McCullogh, M.E., S.D. Kilpatrick, R.A. Emmons and D.B. Larson (2001), 'Is gratitude a moral affect?', *Psychological Bulletin*, **127** (2), 249–66.

McMahon, Darrin (2006), *Happiness: A History*, New York: Atlantic Monthly Press.

Mehrabian, Albert and James A. Russell (1974), *An Approach to Environmental Psychology*, Cambridge, MA: MIT Press.

Miceli, M. and C. Castelfranchi (1998), 'How to silence one's conscience: cognitive defenses against the feeling of guilt', *Journal for the Theory of Social Behaviour*, **28** (3), 287–318.

Mittal, V. and W.A. Kamakura (2001), 'Satisfaction, repurchase intention, and repurchase behaviour: investigating the moderating effect of customer characteristics', *Journal of Marketing Research*, **38** (1), 131–42.

Morales, A.C. (2005), 'Giving firms an "E" for effort: consumer responses to high effort firms', *Journal of Consumer Research*, **31** (4), 806–12.

Nyer, U. (1997), 'A study of the relationships between cognitive appraisals and consumption emotions', *Journal of Academy of Marketing Science*, **25** (4), 296–304.

Oatley, Keith (1992), *Best Laid Schemes: The Psychology of Emotion*, Cambridge, UK: Cambridge University Press.

O'Grady, M. (2006), 'Just inducing fear of HIV/AIDS is not just', *Journal of Health Communication*, **11** (3), 261–2.

O'Shaughnessy, John and Nicholas J. O'Shaughnessy (2003), *The Marketing Power of Emotion*, New York: Oxford University Press.

Oliver, R.L. (1980), 'A cognitive model of the antecedents and consequences of satisfaction decision', *Journal of Marketing Research*, **17** (11), 460–69.

Oliver, R.L. and J.E. Swan (1989), 'Consumer perceptions of interpersonal equity and satisfaction in transactions: a field survey approach', *Journal of Marketing*, **53** (2), 21–35.

Ortony, Andrew, Gerald L. Clore and Allan Collins (1988), *The Cognitive Structure of Emotions*, Cambridge, UK: Cambridge University Press.

Otnes, C., T.M. Lowrey and L.J. Shrum (1997), 'Toward an understanding of consumer ambivalence', *Journal of Consumer Research*, **24** (1), 80–93.

Palmatier, R.W., C.B. Jarvis, J.R. Bechkoff and F.R. Kardes (2009), 'The role of customer gratitude in relationship marketing', *Journal of Marketing*, **73** (5), 1–18.

Parrott, W.G. (2002), 'The functional utility of negative emotions', in Lisa Feldman Barrett, Peter Salovey and John D. Mayer (eds), *The Wisdom in Feeling*, New York: The Guilford Press, pp. 341–59.

Patrick, V.M., H.H. Chun and D.J. MacInnis (2009), 'Affective forecasting and self-control: why anticipating pride wins over anticipating shame in self-regulation context', *Journal of Consumer Psychology*, **19** (3), 537–45.

Patrick, V.M., D.J. MacInnis and V.S. Folkes (2002), 'Approaching what we hope for and avoiding what we fear: the role of possible selves in consumer behavior', *Advances in Consumer Research*, **29**, 270–75.

Pavelchak, M.A., J.H. Antil and J.M. Munch (1988), 'The Super Bowl: an investigation into the relationship among program context, emotional experience, and ad recall', *Journal of Consumer Research*, **15** (3), 360–67.

References

Pham, M.T., J.B. Cohen, J.W. Pracejus and G.D. Hughes (2001), 'Affect monitoring and the primacy of feelings in judgment', *Journal of Consumer Research*, **28** (2), 167–88.

Plutchik, Robert (1962), *The Emotions: The Facts, Theories, and a New Model*, New York: Random House.

Porath, C., D. MacInnis and V. Folkes (2010), 'Witnessing incivility among employees: effects on consumer anger and negative inferences about companies', *Journal of Consumer Research*, **37** (2), 292–303.

Raggio, R.D. and J.A. Garretson Folse (2009), 'Gratitude works: its impact and the mediating role of affective commitment in driving positive outcomes', *Journal of the Academy of Marketing Science*, **37** (4), 455–69.

Raghunathan, R. and K. Corfman (2006), 'Is happiness shared doubled and sadness shared halved? Social influence on enjoyment of hedonic experiences', *Journal of Marketing Research*, **43** (3), 386–94.

Raghunathan, R. and J.R. Irwin (2001), 'Walking the hedonic product treadmill: default contrast and mood-based assimilation in judgments of predicted happiness with a target product', *Journal of Consumer Research*, **28** (3), 355–68.

Raghunathan, R., M.T. Pham and K.P. Corfman (2006), 'Informational properties of anxiety and sadness, and displaced coping', *Journal of Consumer Research*, **32** (4), 596–601.

Rayna, T. and L. Striukova (2009), 'Luxury without guilt: service innovation in the all-inclusive hotel industry', *Service Business*, **3** (4), 359–72.

Richins, M. (1987), 'A multivariate analysis of responses to dissatisfaction', *Journal of Academy of Marketing Science*, **15** (4), 24–31.

Richins, M.L. and S. Dawson (1992), 'A consumer values orientation for materialism and its measurement: scale development and validation', *Journal of Consumer Research*, **19** (3), 303–16.

Rindfleisch, A., J.E. Burroughs and F. Denton (1997), 'Family structure, materialism, and compulsive consumption', *Journal of Consumer Research*, **23** (4), 312–25.

Rindfleisch, A., D. Freeman and J.E. Burroughs (2000), 'Nostalgia, materialism, and product preferences: an initial inquiry', *Advances in Consumer Research*, **27** (1), 36–41.

Roberts, J.A., J.F. Tanner Jr and C. Manolis (2005), 'Materialism and the family structure–stress relation', *Journal of Consumer Psychology*, **15** (2), 183–90.

Roger, R.W. (1983), 'Cognitive and physiological processes in fear appeals and attitude change: a revised theory of protection motivation', in John Cacioppo and Richard Petty (eds), *Social Psychophysiology*, New York: Guilford Press, pp. 153–76.

Romani, S., S. Grappi and D. Dalli (2012), 'Emotions that drive consumers away from brands: measuring negative emotions toward brands and their behavioral effects', *International Journal of Research in Marketing*, **29** (1), 55–67.

Roseman, I.J. (1991), 'Appraisal determinants of discrete emotions', *Cognition and Emotion*, **5** (3), 161–200.

Roseman, I.J. and C.A. Smith (2001), 'Appraisal theory. Overview, assumptions, varieties, controversies', in Klaus R. Scherer, Angela Schorr and T. Johnstone (eds), *Appraisal Processes in Emotion*, Oxford, UK: Oxford University Press.

Roseman, I.J., A.A. Antoniou and P.E. Jose (1996), 'Appraisal determinants of emotions: constructing a more accurate and comprehensive theory', *Cognition and Emotion*, **10** (3), 241–77.

Rust, R.T., J.J. Inman, J. Jia and A. Zahorik (1999), 'What you don't know about customer perceived quality: the role of customer expectation distributions', *Marketing Science*, **18** (1), 77–92.

Ruvio, A. and R.P. Bagozzi (2011), 'The influence of communicator pride and hubris on product evaluations and purchase likelihood', working paper, University of Michigan.

Sabini, John and Maury Silver (eds) (1998), *Emotion, Character, and Responsibility*, New York: Oxford University Press.

Salimpoor, V.N., M. Benovoy, K. Larcher, A. Dagher and R.J. Zatorre (2011), 'Anatomically distinct dopamine release during anticipation and experience of peak emotion to music', *Nature Neuroscience*, **14** (2), 257–62.

Sanchez-Garcia, I. and R. Curras-Perez (2011), 'Effects of dissatisfaction in tourist services: the role of anger and regret', *Tourism Management*, **32** (6), 1397–406.

Scherer, K.R. (1988), 'Criteria for emotion-antecedent appraisal: a review' in V. Hamilton, G.H. Bower and N.H. Frijda (eds), *Cognitive Perspectives on Emotion and Motivation*, Dordrecht: Kluwer, pp. 89–126.

Scherer, K.R. (1993), 'Studying the emotion-antecedent appraisal process: an expert system approach', *Cognition and Emotion*, **7** (4), 325–55.

Shaver, P., J. Schwartz, D. Kirson and C. O'Connor (1987), 'Emotion knowledge: further exploration of a prototype approach', *Journal of Personality and Social Psychology*, **52** (6), 1061–86.

Simonson, I., Z. Carmon, R. Dhar, A. Drolet and S.M. Nowlis (2001), 'Consumer research: in search of identity', *Annual Review of Psychology*, **52**, 249–75.

Singh, J. (1990), 'Voice, exit, and negative word-of-mouth behaviors: an investigation across three service categories', *Journal of Academy of Marketing Science*, **18** (1), 1–15.

Singh, J. and R.E. Wilkes (1996), 'When consumers complain: a path analysis of the key antecedents of consumer complaint response estimates', *Journal of Academy of Marketing Science*, **24** (4), 350–67.

Sirgy, J.M. (1984), 'A social cognition model of CS/D: an experiment', *Psychology & Marketing*, **1**, 27–44.

Skinner, E.A., K. Edge, J. Altman and H. Sherwood (2003), 'Searching for the structure of coping: a review and critique of category systems for classifying ways of coping', *Psychological Bulletin*, **129** (2), 216–69.

Smith, C.A. and P.C. Ellsworth (1985), 'Patterns of cognitive appraisals in emotion', *Journal of Personality and Social Psychology*, **48** (4), 813–38.

Solomon, M.R. (1983), 'The role of products as social stimuli: a symbolic interactionism perspective', *Journal of Consumer Research*, **10** (3), 319–29.

Soscia, I. (2007), 'Gratitude, delight or guilt: the role of consumers' emotions in predicting post-consumption behaviors', *Psychology & Marketing*, **24** (10), 871–94.

Soscia, I. and A. Turrini (2006), 'Sense and sensibility? A study of the role of emotions for customer satisfaction in arts consumption', Università Bocconi, unpublished working paper.

Soscia, I., B. Busacca and E. Pitrelli (2007), 'Guilt decreasing marketing communication: an unexplored appeal', *European Advances in Consumer Research*, **8**, 107–8.

Soscia, I., A. Turrini and E. Tanzi (2012), 'Non Castigat Ridendo Mores: evaluating the effectiveness of humor appeal in printed advertisements for HIV/AIDS prevention in Italy', *Journal of Health Communication*, **17** (9), 1011–27.

Spence, H.E. and R. Moinpour (1972), 'Fear appeal in marketing. A social perspective', *Journal of Marketing*, **36** (3), July, 39–43.

Stearns, Frederic, R. (1972), *Anger. Psychology, Physiology, Pathology*, Springfield, IL: Charles C. Thomas.

Stephens, N. and K.P. Gwinner (1998), 'Why don't some people complain? A cognitive-emotive process model of consumer complaint behaviour', *Journal of Academy of Marketing Science*, **26** (3), 172–89.

Stingo, R. and F. Gallucci (2007), 'Biofeedback and eyetracking: the emotional and cognitive experience in store', *ESOMAR*, 10–23.

Tangney, June P. and Ronda L. Dearing (2002), *Shame and Guilt*, London: The Guilford Press.

Tanner, J.F., J.B. Hunt Jr. and D.R. Eppright (1991), 'The protection motivation model: a normative model for fear appeals', *Journal of Marketing*, **55** (3), 36–45.

Tse, D.K. and P.C. Wilton (1988), 'Model of consumer satisfaction: an extension', *Journal of Marketing Research*, **25** (2), 204–12.

Tsiros, M. and V. Mittal (2000), 'Regret: a model of its antecedents and consequences in consumer decision making', *Journal of Consumer Research*, **26** (4), 401–17.

Tugade, M.M. and B.L. Fredrickson (2002), *Positive Emotions and Emotional Intelligence*, in Lisa Feldman Barrett, Peter Salovey and John D. Mayer (eds), *The Wisdom in Feeling*, New York: The Guilford Press, pp. 319–40.

Ursavas, B. and O. Hesapçı-Sanaktekin (2011), 'What happens when you're lost between happiness and sadness?', *Journal of Business Research*, doi:10.1016.

Vaughn, R. (1980), 'How advertising works: a planning model', *Journal of Advertising Research*, **20** (5), 27–33.

Veling, H., K.I. Ruys and A. Henk (2011), 'Anger as a hidden motivator: associating attainable products with anger turns them into rewards', *Social Psychological and Personality Science*, November, doi: 10.1177/1948550611425425.

Wang, J. (2006), 'The politics of goods: a case study of consumer nationalism and media discourse in contemporary China', *Asian Journal of Communication*, **16** (2), 187–206.

Wang, J. and Z. Wang (2007), 'The political symbolism of business. Exploring consumer nationalism and its implications for corporate reputation management in China', *Journal of Communication Management*, **11** (2), 134–49.

Wansink, B. and P. Chandon (2006), 'Can "low-fat" nutrition labels lead to obesity?', *Journal of Marketing Research*, **43** (4), 605–17.

Watkins, Philip, C. (2004), 'Gratitude and subjective well-being', in Robert A. Emmons and Michael E. McCullough (eds), *The Psychology of Gratitude*, New York: Oxford University Press, pp. 167–92.

Watson, D. and A. Tellegen (1985), 'Toward a consensual structure of mood', *Psychological Bulletin*, **98** (2), 219–35.

Weiner, B. (1985), 'An attributional theory of achievement motivation and emotion', *Psychological Review*, **92** (4), 548–73.

Westbrook, R.A. and M.D. Reilly (1983), 'Value-percept disparity: an alternative to the disconfirmation and expectations theory of consumer satisfaction', *Advances in Consumer Research*, **10**, 394–8.

Williams, P. and J.L. Aaker (2002), 'Can mixed emotions peacefully coexist?', *Journal of Consumer Research*, **28** (4), 636–49.

Wilson, T.D., S. Lindsey and T.Y. Schooler (2000), 'A model of dual attitudes', *Psychological Review*, **107** (1), 101–26.

Woodruff, R.B., E.R. Cadotte and R.L. Jenkins (1983), 'Modeling customer satisfaction processes using experience-based norms', *Journal of Marketing Research*, **20** (3), 296–304.

Yi, S. and V. Baumgartner (2004), 'Coping with negative emotions in purchase-related situations', *Journal of Consumer Psychology*, **14** (3), 303–17.

Yi, Y. (1989), 'A critical review of customer satisfaction', working paper, Division of Research – School of Business Administration – University of Michigan.

Yi, Y. and S. La (2004), 'What influences the relationship between customer satisfaction and repurchase intention? Investigating the effect of adjusted expectation and customer loyalty', *Psychology & Marketing*, **21** (5), 351–73.

Zajonc, R.B. (1980), 'Feeling and thinking. Preferences need no inferences', *American Psychologist*, **35** (2), 151–75.

Index

Aaker, J.L. 2, 34, 73
accusations 55
action tendencies, emotions and 7,
    14–15, 102
  anger 78–80
  gratitude 90–93
  guilt 54–7
  happiness and unhappiness 25–9,
    30
  hope and fear 42
  pride 70–72
adaptation-level theory 47, 73
advertising
  emotions and 2
  fear 43, 45, 46–7
  guilt 58, 60, 61, 63
  happiness/unhappiness 34,
    35
  hope 42, 43, 44
  pride 73
  humour and 46, 47
agency 12
aggravating behaviour 82, 84
Agrawal, N. 66
AIDS 43, 45, 46–7, 61
alternatives 40
altruism 92
anger 15, 22, 65, 78
  cognitive antecedents and action
    tendencies 78–80
  consumer behaviour and 80–90
  predictive model of post-
    purchase behaviour and
    101, 102, 103, 106, 107, 108,
    112
anticipated emotions 8, 20, 57, 72
anxiety 34
apathy 5
apologies 85–6

appeals
  guilt-arousing 60–61, 63
  guilt-decreasing 61, 63
appraisal of emotions
  attributional 86
  happiness 26, 28
  hope 42
  satisfaction 36
arousal 17, 35
attribution judgement 40

Babakus, E. 74
Bagozzi, R.P. 2, 7, 8, 19
Baumeister, R.F. 54
Baumgartner, V. 102
behaviour, see consumer behaviour,
    emotions and
belonging: desire to belong 33
Ben-Ze'ev, A. 3
Benetton 69
Beverland, M.B. 82
binary categories 5
Bonifield, C. 82
Bougie, R. 81, 100, 102
brain scanning 113–14
British Airways 86–7
broken promises 80
Brotherton, T.P. 58
Burnett, M.S. 58, 59

Cadotte, E.R. 36
Cahill, L. 114
Cameron, David 25
care, desire for 33
Castelfranchi, C. 55
causation of events 10, 12, 26, 40,
    100, 101
China 73
Chun, H. 66

classes of emotions 15–19
Cochrane, L. 43
cognitive antecedents of emotions
    7, 9–13, 100
  anger 78–80
  gratitude 90–93
  guilt 54–7
  happiness and unhappiness
    25–9
  hope and fear 42
  pride 70–72
Cole, C. 82
collective nostalgia 49
combinations of emotions 4
compensation 40
competition 40
complaints 40–41, 67, 84, 99, 107
complexity of emotions 4–5
consumer behaviour, emotions and
    19–21
  anger 80–90
  gratitude 93–7
  guilt 58–63
    relationship between guilt,
      shame and embarrassment
      64–70
  happiness/unhappiness 30–35
  predictive model of post-
    purchase behaviour based
    on emotions 21–3, 98
    derivation 98–103
    discussion 111–12
    empirical assessment 104–11
    neuroscientific methods
      to study and measure
      emotions 112–15
  pride 72–7
contingency approach 2
controllability 12
coping methods 14–15, 30–31
Corfman, K. 32
corporate social responsibility 61
Cotte, J. 61
Coulter, R.H. 61
coupons 74
Csikszentmihalyi, Mihali 27
cultural differences, emotions and 4

Dahl, D.W. 58, 59, 60, 68, 70
Dallimore, K.S. 84
Dawson, S. 30, 50
Day, R.L. 35–6
De Hooge, I.E. 66
de Mello, G. 42
Dearing, Ronda L. 64, 65, 66
definition of emotions 7
denial 57
desire 36
  desirability of events 10, 11, 100,
    101
  desirable happiness and
    undesirable sadness 41–7
  desire for care 33
  desire to belong 33
direct accusations 55
disagreement 33
discount coupons 74
dissatisfaction 4, 35–7, 40–41, 67,
    80–81, 99
Dolce & Gabbana 69
dominance 17
Donovan, R.J. 1
Drolet, A. 68
Ducati 20
Dufour 34
Duhachek, A. 66
Duke, C.R. 47
duration of emotions 6
Durkheim, Emile 27

education levels 41
Ellsworth, P.C. 28
Elster, Jon 5
embarrassment: relationship
    between guilt, shame and
    embarrassment 64–70
emotions and 2, 3–9
emotive contamination theory 33,
    84
emotive traits 9
empathy 65
epistemic emotions 18–19
equity, perceived 37
Erevelles, S. 2
expectations 36, 100

explanations
  prospective 84–5
  retrospective 84
expressed hostility 80
expression of emotions 55–6

facial expressions, emotions and 6
factive emotions 18
failure, unhappiness and 28–9, 34
fear 42, 43–7, 51–2
Fiat 60
financial guilt 58
Financial Times 68
forgiveness 55
Fredrickson, B.L. 28
Frijda, N.H. 14–15, 64, 102
frustration 78
Funches, V. 80–90
Funk, D.C. 74

Galens Medical Society 60
Garretson Folse, J.A. 95
Gelbrich, K. 84
Germany 90
Gladden, J.M. 74
goals 10–11
Goldberg, M.E. 2
Gorn, G.J. 2
gratitude 78
  cognitive antecedents and
    tendencies to action 90–93
  consumer behaviour and 93–7
  predictive model of post-
    purchase behaviour and 101,
    103, 107, 109, 112
Green, E.C. 45
Greer, S.M. 114
Gucci 61
guilt 23, 54, 76–7
  cognitive antecedents and
    tendencies to action 54–7
  predictive model of post-
    purchase behaviour and 101,
    103, 106, 107, 108, 112
  relationship between guilt,
    shame and embarrassment
    64–70

Halperin, D.T. 45
Hamann, S. 114
happiness 25, 51–2
  cognitive antecedents and
    tendencies to action
    25–8
  consumer behaviour and 30–34,
    35
  desirable 41–7
  gratitude and 92
  nostalgia and memory of
    irretrievable happiness
    47–50
  predictive model of post-
    purchase behaviour and 100,
    101, 106, 112
  satisfaction as lukewarm version
    of 35–41
Hastings, G. 46
hate 79
health guilt 58, 59
Helson, Henry 47, 73
Higgins, E.T. 74
Hirschman, E.C. 17
hope 26–7, 41–3, 44, 47, 51–2
hostility, expressed 80
Hsu, M. 45
hubris 73–4
Huhmann, B.A. 58

imaging techniques 113–14
impoliteness 87, 90
importance of products 41
impulse purchases 1–2
incivility 87, 90
income levels 41
indifference 6
indirect accusations 55
intensity of emotions 11
intention 12
Italy 40, 60
Izard, C.E. 13, 17

Japan 30
JetBlue 84, 85–6
Jiménez, M. 61
joy, *see* happiness

judgement
  of assets 32
  attribution judgement 40

Kant, Immanuel 70
Kirby, D. 45
Knutson, B. 114

Lafeber Company 96
language differences, emotions
    and 4
latent interests 11
Lau-Gesk, L. 68
Lazarus, R.S. 26, 29
Lee, A.Y. 2, 73
life satisfaction 30
loneliness 27
Louro, M.J. 75, 103
love 90
Lunsford, D.A. 58, 59
Lyubomirsky, S. 27

McCullogh, M.E. 91
McGaugh, J.L. 114
MacInnis, D.J. 42
manifest interests 11
Mano, H. 17, 18
marketing, role played by emotions
    in 1–3
materialism 30, 31, 50
Mattila, A.S. 67
measurement of emotions 112–15
Mehrabian, Albert 17, 36
Miceli, M. 55
mixed emotions 17
monopoly 40
moral barometer 92
moral emotion 54
moral guilt 58, 59
moral stimulus 92
moral support 92
Morales, A.C. 93, 94, 103
motivation 12, 13
  protection motivation theory 45–6

national pride 75
neural processes, emotions and 13

neuroscientific methods to study
    and measure emotions 112–15
norms 37
nostalgia 21, 51–2
  memory of irretrievable
      happiness and 47–50
Nyer, U. 100

Oatley, Keith 26, 27, 28, 30
O'Grady, M. 45
oligopoly 40
Oliver, R.L. 17, 18
O'Shaughnessy, John 18, 87
O'Shaughnessy, Nicholas J. 18, 87

Palmatier, R.W. 93, 94
partiality of emotions 6–7
Patek Philippe 59, 63
Patrick, V.M. 72
Pavelchak, M.A. 2
perceived equity 37
personal shoppers 93
personality 9
physiological activation of
    emotions 6
Pinto, M.B. 61
place, pride of 74
pleasure 17, 35
  guilty 63
Plutchik, Robert 17
Porath, C. 87
positivity 20
poverty, unhappiness and 30
predictive model of post-purchase
    behaviour based on emotions
    21–3
  derivation 98–103
  discussion 111–12
  empirical assessment 104–11
  neuroscientific methods to study
      and measure emotions
      112–15
prevention pride 74
pride 54
  cognitive antecedents and action
      tendencies 70–72
  consumer behaviour and 72–7

predictive model of post-
    purchase behaviour and 101,
    109
primary emotions 17
Procter & Gamble 114
product life cycles 2–3
promises, broken 80
promotion pride 74
prospective explanations 84–5
protection motivation theory 45–6
prototype categories 5

Quester, P. 43

Raggio, R.D. 95
Raghunathan, R. 32, 34
rationality 2, 5
regret 23
relationships, happiness and 27
responsibility 80, 103
retrospective explanations 84
Revlon 41
Richins, M.L. 30, 50
Rindfleisch, A. 50
Roberts, J.A. 31
Roseman, I.J. 26, 28, 104
Rossiter, R. 1
Russell, James A. 17, 36

Sabini, John 66
sadness, *see* unhappiness
Salimpoor, V.N. 114
satisfaction 99
    dissatisfaction 4, 35–7, 40–41, 67,
      80–81, 99
    life satisfaction 30
    as lukewarm version of happiness
      35–41
Scherer, K.R. 12
self-control 66
self-esteem 67, 73
self-indulgence 59
shame: relationship between guilt,
    shame and embarrassment
    64–70
Shaver, P. 17, 36
Silver, Maury 66

simulated nostalgia 48–9
Sirgy, J.M. 36
Smith, C.A. 28
social context 32
social emotion 54
social guilt 58, 59
Solomon, M.R. 50
sophistication of consumers 41
Soscia, I. 46
spontaneity of emotions 6–7
Stearns, Frederic 79
Stern, B.B. 17
suicide 25, 64

Taiwan 45
Tangney, June P. 64, 65, 66
Tanner, J.F. 46
Telefono Azzurro 60
television programmes, advertising
    and 2
temperament 8
threats 43
trade-offs 42
Tugade, M.M. 28

'Un Techo para Chile 2011'
    campaign 59
unfair treatment 80
unhappiness (sadness) 25, 30,
    51–2
    cognitive antecedents and
      tendencies to action 28–9
    consumer behaviour and 34
    predictive model of post-
      purchase behaviour and 100,
      101, 102, 106, 107, 108, 112
    undesirable sadness 41–7
United Kingdom 25
United States of America
    gratitude in 90
    happiness in 27, 30
    pride in 73

Veling, H. 90

Weiner, B. 12, 28
Williams, P. 34

Wirtz, J. 67

withdrawal, unhappiness and 29

Witte, K. 45

women 105
    unhappiness and 34

Woodruff, R.B. 36

Woodstock 48

Yang, K.C.C. 61

Yi, S. 102

Zales Diamonds 20